YOUR recipe could appear in our next cookbook!

Share your tried & true family favorites with us instantly at
www.gooseberrypatch.com
If you'd rather jot 'em down by hand, just mail this form to...
Gooseberry Patch • Cookbooks – Call for Recipes
PO Box 812 • Columbus, OH 43216-0812

If your recipe is selected for a book, you'll receive a FREE copy!

Please share only your original recipes or those that you have made your own over the years.

Recipe Name:

Number of Servings:

Any fond memories about this recipe? Special touches you like to add
or handy shortcuts?

Ingredients (include specific measurements):

Instructions (continue on back if needed):

Special Code: **cookbookspage**

Over ↗

Extra space for recipe if needed:

Tell us about yourself...

Your complete contact information is needed so that we can send you your FREE cookbook, if your recipe is published. Phone numbers and email addresses are kept private and will only be used if we have questions about your recipe.

Name:

Address:

City: State: Zip:

Email:

Daytime Phone:

Thank you! Vickie & Jo Ann

Gooseberry Patch

An imprint of Globe Pequot
246 Goose Lane
Guilford, CT 06437

www.gooseberrypatch.com

1•800•854•6673

Copyright 2010, Gooseberry Patch 978-1-62093-241-4

Photo Edition is a major revision of *Homestyle in a Hurry.*

Do you have a tried & true recipe...

tip, craft or memory that you'd like to see featured in a **Gooseberry Patch** cookbook? Visit our website at **www.gooseberrypatch.com** and follow the easy steps to submit your favorite family recipe. Or send them to us at:

Gooseberry Patch
PO Box 812
Columbus, OH 43216-0812

Don't forget to include the number of servings your recipe makes, plus your name, address, phone number and email address. If we select your recipe, your name will appear right along with it... and you'll receive a **FREE** copy of the book!

Contents

Dedication

To families large & small who look forward to sharing home-cooked meals together, no matter how busy they are!

Appreciation

To all our friends who shared a favorite, tried & true recipe...our heartiest thanks!

Busy-Day
Breakfasts

Morning Mix-Up

Mary Patenaude
Griswold, CT

*Add a basket of warm muffins and a side of
fresh fruit...breakfast is served!*

2 c. frozen diced potatoes
1 c. cooked ham, chopped
1/2 c. onion, chopped
2 T. oil

6 eggs, beaten
salt and pepper to taste
1 c. shredded Cheddar cheese

In a large skillet over medium heat, sauté potatoes, ham and onion in oil for 10 minutes, or until potatoes are tender. Whisk eggs with salt and pepper. Reduce heat to low; add eggs to skillet. Cook, stirring occasionally, until eggs are set. Remove from heat and gently stir in cheese. Serves 4.

Egg dishes are a terrific way to use up tasty tidbits
from the fridge...ham, deli meats, chopped veggies and
cheese. Warm ingredients briefly in a skillet and scramble
the eggs right in, or make a hearty overstuffed omelet.

Kicked-Up Eggs

Beckie Apple
Grannis, AR

My family's favorite weekend breakfast...everyone loves it!
Toasted English muffins with butter and jam complete the meal.

1/4 c. butter
1 c. cooked ham, diced
1 onion, chopped
1 green pepper, chopped
4-oz. can sliced mushrooms,
   drained

10 eggs
1/2 t. salt
1/2 t. pepper
8-oz. pkg. shredded Cheddar
   cheese

In a large, deep skillet, melt butter over medium heat. Add ham, onion, green pepper and mushrooms. Cook for 5 minutes, stirring often. Reduce heat to low; add eggs, salt and pepper. Do not stir for 2 minutes so egg whites can set. After 2 minutes, stir egg mixture and add cheese. Continue cooking, stirring gently, until eggs are softly scrambled. Makes 6 to 8 servings.

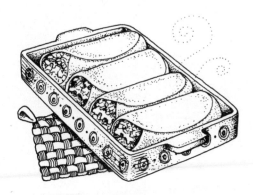

Are family members eating breakfast on the run?
Any egg dish turns into a portable breakfast when
rolled up in a tortilla or spooned into a pita round.

California Omelet

Christina Mendoza
Alamogordo, NM

I enjoyed trying a similar omelet in El Cajon, California once while visiting my cousin there. I just had to try my hand at making my own version of it...this is the yummy result!

1 T. oil
3 to 4 eggs, beaten
1/4 c. milk
salt and pepper to taste
1 avocado, pitted, peeled
   and sliced

2 to 3 green onions, diced
1/2 c. shredded Monterey Jack
   cheese

Heat oil in a skillet over medium-low heat. In a bowl, whisk eggs with milk, salt and pepper; pour into skillet. Cook until eggs are lightly golden on bottom and partially set on top. Sprinkle with remaining ingredients; carefully fold omelet in half so toppings are covered. Reduce heat to medium-low and cook, uncovered, about 10 minutes. Serves 2.

We love breakfast foods, but it seems like there's
never time to linger over them in the morning. Enjoy an
unhurried breakfast with your family...at dinnertime!
An omelet or frittata is perfect. Just add a basket of
muffins, fresh fruit and a steamy pot of tea.

Scrambled Eggs Deluxe

Marla Raines
San Angelo, TX

So much more delicious than plain old scrambled eggs!

1 lb. bacon, cut into bite-size
    pieces
10 eggs, beaten

8-oz. pkg. cream cheese, cubed
    and softened
salt and pepper to taste

Place bacon in a large skillet over medium heat. Cook until almost crisp. Reduce heat to low; add eggs and cream cheese. Cook until eggs are set. Season eggs with salt and pepper. Makes 4 to 6 servings.

For savory egg dishes, a windowsill herb garden
is terrific. Mini pots of thyme, marjoram and chives
don't need much care...and they're always handy
to pinch off and add as you cook.

Eggs à la Goldenrod

Beckie Butcher
Elgin, IL

A true comfort food...day or night! My grandmother used to make these eggs for my mother every Saturday morning. Many years later, whenever my mother could tell I'd had a tough day, she would make this dish for me as a special dinner to cheer me up.

2 T. butter
2 T. all-purpose flour
1/2 t. salt
pepper to taste
1/3 c. evaporated milk

2/3 c. water
2 eggs, hard-boiled, peeled
   and halved
3 slices bread, toasted
Garnish: paprika

Melt butter in a saucepan over medium heat. In a bowl, mix flour, salt and pepper; stir into butter. Combine milk and water. Gradually pour milk mixture over butter mixture, stirring until smooth. Separate egg whites and yolks. Finely chop whites and add to mixture in skillet; spread on toast. Mash yolks with a fork and sprinkle on top of toast. Sprinkle with paprika. Makes 3 servings.

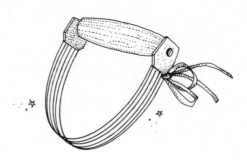

Chop up hard-boiled eggs for a recipe in a jiffy...just use a pastry blender.

Busy-Day Breakfasts

Sausage Breakfast Pizza

Audrey Lett
Newark, DE

My kids were such fussy eaters in the morning...until I let them have pizza for breakfast! Now they love to help make our breakfast pizzas and even think up new toppings to add.

1 lb. ground pork sausage
1 c. sliced mushrooms
13.8-oz. tube refrigerated pizza
  dough
1 c. tomatoes, diced
2 c. shredded pizza-blend
  cheese
4 eggs, beaten

In a skillet over medium heat, cook sausage and mushrooms until browned; drain. Unroll dough and press into a greased 13"x9" baking pan, covering bottom of pan and 2 inches up sides. Top dough with sausage mixture, tomatoes and cheese; pour eggs over top. Bake, uncovered, at 400 degrees for 13 to 15 minutes, or until crust is golden and eggs are set. Makes 6 to 8 servings.

A fresh, fun side for breakfast...fruit kabobs! Just slide juicy strawberries, pineapple chunks, kiwi fruit slices and orange wedges onto wooden skewers.

Babci's Doughnut French Toast
Barbara Cebula
Chicopee, MA

Babci was my grandmother from my mother's side and she meant the world to me. She used to take me to the hat shop and to Mass. She even taught me how to sing and speak in Polish. Babci would make this recipe for us whenever we spent the weekend with her.

2 eggs, beaten
1/4 c. milk
4 t. vanilla extract
4 slices white bread, halved

2 T. butter
1 to 2 T. oil
1/4 c. powdered sugar

Beat eggs with milk and vanilla in a wide, shallow bowl. Soak bread in egg mixture for 5 minutes per side. Heat butter and oil in a skillet over medium heat. Fry egg-soaked bread until golden on both sides. Put powdered sugar on a plate; dredge cooked bread until coated like a sugary doughnut. Serve warm. Makes 2 servings.

Honey Butter
Jill Ball
Highland, UT

My family loves to eat this extra-special honey butter on warm toast or rolls...or just with a spoon!

1 c. butter, softened
1 c. honey

7-oz. jar marshmallow creme
1/2 t. vanilla extract

Combine all ingredients in a food processor; process until mixed. Store in a covered bowl. Makes about 3 cups.

Busy-Day
Breakfasts

Megan's Cinnamon Pancakes
Megan Dulgarian
Moore, OK

These pancakes fill the house with a sweet cinnamon smell. We love to make them for breakfast on special occasions, especially in chilly weather. We've even enjoyed them for dessert once or twice!

1-1/2 c. all-purpose flour
3-1/2 t. baking powder
1 t. salt
1 T. sugar
1 t. cinnamon
1-1/4 c. milk

1 egg, beaten
2 T. vanilla extract
3 T. butter, melted and slightly cooled
1/3 c. cinnamon baking chips

In a large bowl, sift together flour, baking powder, salt, sugar and cinnamon. Add milk, egg, vanilla and melted butter; mix until smooth. Fold in cinnamon chips. Lightly grease a griddle or frying pan and heat over medium-high heat. Pour batter onto heated griddle by 1/4 cupfuls. Cook until golden on both sides. Serve warm with Cream Cheese Topping. Makes one dozen pancakes.

Cream Cheese Topping:

1/2 c. cream cheese, softened
1/4 c. butter, softened
1 c. powdered sugar

1/2 t. vanilla extract
1/4 t. lemon juice
2 T. milk

Beat together cream cheese and butter until smooth. Add remaining ingredients; mix until well blended. Serve at room temperature or warmed. May be stored in refrigerator for up to one week.

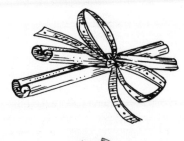

Quick Poppy Seed Muffins

Brenda Trnka
Manitoba, Canada

Such an easy recipe! These are terrific at breakfast,
with tea or for after-school snacks.

18-1/4 oz. pkg. lemon cake mix   1/2 c. poppy seed
   with pudding   Garnish: sugar

Prepare cake batter according to package directions. Add poppy seed;
mix well. Fill greased muffin cups 2/3 full. Top each muffin with a
sprinkle of sugar. Bake at 350 degrees for about 8 to 10 minutes,
until muffins test done. Makes 2 dozen muffins.

Orange Blossom Honey Butter

Sharon Demers
Dolores, CO

This is so yummy spread on hot muffins...what a treat!

1/2 c. butter, softened   1 T. orange zest
2 T. honey

In a small bowl, beat butter until light and fluffy. Beat in honey and
orange zest until well blended. Cover and refrigerate. Makes 1/2 cup.

For orange zest in a jiffy, use a vegetable peeler to remove
very thin slices of peel. Mince finely with a paring knife.

Busy-Day Breakfasts

Cherries & Cream Muffins

Jodi Griggs
Richmond, KY

*These sweet muffins sparkle with sugar topping
and taste oh-so delightful!*

1/2 c. butter, softened
1 c. sugar
2 eggs, beaten
1 t. almond extract
1/2 t. vanilla extract
2-1/2 c. frozen unsweetened
    tart cherries, thawed, drained
    and divided

2 c. all-purpose flour
2 t. baking powder
1/2 t. salt
1/2 c. milk, divided
Garnish: sugar

In a large bowl, beat butter and sugar until light and fluffy. Add eggs
and extracts; blend well. Add half of the cherries to batter; set aside.
Combine flour, baking powder and salt in a separate bowl. Add half
of the flour mixture to butter mixture with a spatula, then half of the
milk. Add remaining flour mixture and milk; mix well. Fold in
remaining cherries. Fill greased muffin cups 2/3 full. Sprinkle
generously with sugar. Bake at 375 degrees for 20 to 30 minutes,
until golden. Makes one dozen muffins.

It takes just minutes to
make breakfast fun for kids,
especially on school days.
Cut the centers from a slice
of toast with a cookie cutter,
serve milk or juice with twisty
straws or put a smiley face on
a bagel using raisins and
cream cheese.

Morning Glory Muffins

Michelle Campen
Peoria, IL

You'll love these yummy muffins like I do...they're packed with good-for-you ingredients!

2 c. all-purpose flour
1-1/4 c. sugar
2 t. baking soda
1/2 t. salt
2 t. cinnamon
2 c. carrots, peeled and grated
1 c. apple, cored, peeled and chopped
1/2 c. raisins
1/2 c. unsalted sunflower kernels
1/2 c. sweetened flaked coconut
3 eggs, beaten
1 c. oil
2 t. vanilla extract

In a large bowl, combine flour, sugar, baking soda, salt and cinnamon. Stir in carrots, apple, raisins, sunflower kernels and coconut. In a separate bowl, whisk together eggs, oil and vanilla; stir into flour mixture until batter is just combined. Let batter rest for 4 minutes. Spoon into well-greased muffin cups, filling 2/3 full. Bake at 350 degrees for 20 to 25 minutes. Let muffins cool in tin for 10 minutes. Turn out onto a wire rack to finish cooling. Makes 16 muffins.

Use an old-fashioned ice cream scoop to fill muffin cups with batter...no spills, no drips and the muffins turn out perfectly sized!

Busy-Day Breakfasts

Speedy Sausage Muffins

Lisa Gibbs
Nashville, TN

My mother-in-law bakes these muffins for us. She serves them with hot coffee and spiced tea...so nice on a cool morning!

1 lb. ground pork sausage,
  browned and drained
3 c. biscuit baking mix
1-1/2 c. shredded Cheddar
  cheese

10-3/4 oz. can Cheddar cheese
  soup
3/4 c. water

Combine sausage, baking mix and cheese in a large bowl; make a well in center of mixture. Stir together soup and water; add to sausage mixture, stirring just until combined. Spoon into lightly greased muffin cups, filling to top of cups. Bake at 375 degrees for 20 to 25 minutes, until lightly golden. Serve warm. Makes 16 muffins.

Invite a best girlfriend over for a Saturday morning brunch...a great way for the two of you to spend time catching up!

Oh-So-Easy Biscuits

Beverly Brewer
Tulsa, OK

I could never make good biscuits until this recipe was shared with me
by a co-worker. These are wonderful...and, most of all, easy!

2-1/2 c. self-rising flour   Optional: milk, bacon drippings
1 pt. whipping cream

Place flour and cream in a bowl. Stir until dough forms; add a little
milk if too dry. Place on a floured board; knead until dough is
consistent. Divide dough into 12 parts; roll each into a ball and pat
with flour to flatten a little. Place on an ungreased baking sheet. Brush
tops with bacon drippings, if desired. Bake at 450 degrees for 10 to
15 minutes, until golden. Makes about one dozen biscuits.

Country Sausage Gravy

JoAnn

Can't beat this recipe for sausage gravy. So yummy with fresh-baked
biscuits...a quick & easy breakfast everyone will love!

1 lb. ground pork sausage   1-1/2 c. water
1/4 c. butter   salt and pepper to taste
1/4 c. all-purpose flour   6 biscuits, split
12-oz. can evaporated milk

Brown sausage in a skillet over medium-high heat; drain. Melt butter
in skillet; add flour and cook for one minute, stirring constantly.
Combine evaporated milk and water. Gradually add to mixture in
skillet, stirring constantly. Bring to a boil. Reduce heat to low and
cook until thickened, stirring occasionally. Season with salt and
pepper. Serve gravy spooned over split biscuits. Serves 6.

Cozy Breakfast Casserole

Patty Hiner
New River, AZ

This is our favorite weekend breakfast & brunch meal. If you prefer, use browned ground pork sausage instead of links...even add diced onions and green peppers.

3 lbs. potatoes, peeled
  and cubed
2 T. oil
salt and pepper to taste
1 lb. bacon, crisply cooked
  and crumbled

1 lb. smoked pork sausage
  links, browned and cut into
  bite-size pieces
1/2 lb. cooked ham, cubed
2 c. shredded Cheddar cheese

In a large skillet over medium heat, cook potatoes in oil until golden. Season with salt and pepper. Add remaining ingredients except cheese; reduce heat. Cover and cook for about 15 minutes, or until potatoes are tender, stirring occasionally. Transfer to a greased 13"x9" baking pan. Add cheese and mix. Bake, uncovered, at 350 degrees for 10 minutes, or until cheese is melted. Serves 8 to 10.

Get the day off to a great start...put together a hearty breakfast casserole and refrigerate. The next morning, just pop it in the oven.

Ham Skillet Breakfast

Barbara Bledsoe
Saint Louis, MO

Super quick...you don't even have to peel the potatoes!

2 potatoes, cubed
1 onion, chopped
2 to 3 T. oil
1 green pepper, chopped

1 zucchini, chopped
2 c. cooked ham, diced
1 tomato, diced
1/2 c. shredded Cheddar cheese

In a large skillet over medium-high heat, cook potatoes and onion in oil for 5 minutes, or until golden. Add green pepper and zucchini. Cook for 5 additional minutes, until tender. Add ham and tomato; sprinkle with cheese. Cover and cook for 3 to 5 minutes, until heated through and cheese melts. Serves 4.

Butter-flavored non-stick vegetable spray is especially handy at breakfast time...use it to spray a skillet for cooking eggs, a waffle iron, pancake griddle or baking pan.

Easy Bacon Frittata

Beth Bundy
Long Prairie, MN

Delicious and so simple to put together! Pair it with fruit salad for brunch or a crisp green salad for an easy dinner.

2 c. frozen shredded
   hashbrowns
3 T. oil
7 eggs, beaten

2 T. milk
12 slices bacon, crisply cooked
   and crumbled
3/4 c. shredded Cheddar cheese

Add hashbrowns and oil to a large skillet over medium heat. Cook for 10 to 15 minutes, stirring often, until potatoes are golden; drain. In a separate bowl, whisk together eggs and milk. Pour egg mixture over potatoes; sprinkle with bacon. Cover and reduce heat to low. Cook 10 minutes longer, or until eggs are set. Sprinkle with cheese; cover again and cook about 5 minutes, until cheese is melted. Cut into wedges to serve. Makes 6 servings.

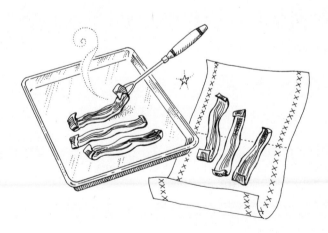

Save time and clean-up...bake the bacon! Arrange slices on a jelly-roll pan. Bake at 350 degrees for 15 to 20 minutes, until done to desired crispness. Drain well on paper towels.

Pigs in the Clover

Cathy Nign
Temple City, CA

*My Norwegian mother-in-law gave me this recipe. She told me
this was a dish she ate while growing up.*

14-3/4 oz. can creamed corn
2 to 3 potatoes, peeled, boiled
  and cubed

salt and pepper to taste
8 pork breakfast sausage links,
  browned

Pour creamed corn into a greased 8"x8" baking pan. Place potatoes
over corn; sprinkle with salt and pepper. Arrange sausage links on
top. Cover with aluminum foil. Bake at 350 degrees for 30 minutes, or
until hot and bubbly. Serves 4 to 6.

Ham & Cheese Crescents

LaRica Krischel
Edmond, OK

*One day I was experimenting with what we had in the fridge,
and I came up with this easy recipe...my husband, daughter
and I think it's a winner!*

2 8-oz. tubes refrigerated
  crescent rolls
9-oz. pkg. sliced deli ham,
  chopped

16-oz. pkg. favorite shredded
  cheese

Layer one tube of crescent rolls in the bottom of a greased 8"x8"
baking pan. Pinch rolls together to form a crust. Layer ham and
cheese on top of rolls. Add remaining tube of rolls over cheese,
pinching rolls together to form the top layer. Bake at 375 degrees for
20 minutes, or until golden on top. Serves 6 to 8.

Sour Cream Scones

Elaine Anderson
Aliquippa, FL

Bake up some tender scones with ingredients you probably already have on hand. Serve with butter and jam...yum!

2 c. all-purpose flour
2 t. baking powder
1/2 t. baking soda
1/2 t. salt

1/4 c. butter
2 eggs, beaten
1/2 c. sour cream

Combine flour, baking powder, baking soda and salt; cut in butter until mixture resembles coarse crumbs. In a separate bowl, mix eggs and sour cream; stir into flour mixture until dough leaves the sides of the bowl. Knead for one minute. On a floured surface, roll out dough into a 9-inch by 6-inch rectangle. Cut into 6, 3-inch by 3-inch squares; cut each square diagonally. Arrange scones on an ungreased baking sheet, 2 inches apart. Bake at 400 degrees for 10 to 12 minutes. Makes one dozen.

Creamery "Butter"

Angie Stone
Argillite, KY

We call this "country butter without the cow"!

16-oz. pkg. margarine, softened
8-oz. pkg. cream cheese,
    softened

5-oz. can evaporated milk

Blend all ingredients until smooth and creamy. Cover and chill before serving; keep refrigerated. Makes about 3 cups.

Rock Buns

Clare Adams
Tyler Hill, PA

These are very delicious! They are my favorite recipe for scones, shared by a friend who came from South Africa. I use a stand mixer to make this very easy.

4 c. all-purpose flour
3/4 c. butter
1 c. sugar
1 T. baking powder
1 c. sweetened flaked coconut

1 c. dried fruit bits or currants
2 eggs, beaten
1 t. vanilla extract
1/3 c. milk

Place flour in a large bowl. With a stand mixer or 2 knives, cut in butter until mixture resembles fine crumbs. Mix in sugar, baking powder, coconut and fruit. In a separate bowl, combine eggs, vanilla and milk; add to flour mixture, stirring to blend. Form dough into buns by 1/4 cupfuls; place on lightly greased baking sheets, about 2 inches apart. Bake at 400 degrees for 15 to 18 minutes, until golden. Makes about one dozen.

Make quick & easy freezer preserves to enjoy at breakfast. Combine one pound ripe strawberries, 1-1/2 cups sugar and 2 tablespoons lemon juice. Bring to a boil, lower heat and simmer, uncovered, for 30 minutes. Spoon into sterilized freezer containers; keep frozen for up to 6 months.

Buttery Coffee Cake

Suzette Howell
Newcastle, OK

A quick & easy dessert that's scrumptious with a cup of coffee.

18-1/4 oz. pkg. butter cake mix
1/2 c. butter, melted and slightly
  cooled
4 eggs, beaten and divided

8-oz. pkg. cream cheese,
  softened
2 c. powdered sugar

In a large bowl, mix together dry cake mix, butter and half of eggs. Pour into an ungreased, floured 8"x8" baking pan; set aside. In a separate bowl, blend together remaining eggs, cream cheese and powdered sugar. Spoon cream cheese mixture over cake batter. Bake at 350 degrees for 20 to 25 minutes. Makes 9 servings.

Having friends over for breakfast or brunch?
Set the table the night before...one less thing
to think about in the morning!

Berry Bubble Coffee Cake

Katie Foster
Indianola, NE

I tried this recipe one weekend when we had company. It quickly became an easy-to-make favorite.

1/4 c. butter, melted
1/2 c. brown sugar, packed
8-oz. tube refrigerated biscuits,
 quartered
1/2 t. cinnamon

1 c. quick-cooking oats,
 uncooked and divided
1-1/2 c. frozen mixed berries,
 thawed
1/2 c. sugar

Place melted butter and brown sugar in separate small bowls. Dip each biscuit quarter into butter and then into brown sugar. Arrange biscuits in a single layer in a greased 8"x8" baking pan. Sprinkle evenly with cinnamon; top with half the oats. Toss together berries and sugar in a bowl; spoon evenly over oats. Sprinkle remaining oats over berries. If there is any remaining butter, drizzle it on top. Bake at 375 degrees for 20 minutes, or until golden. Cool for 15 minutes before serving. Serves 8.

Add a dash of whimsy to the breakfast table...serve up cream or pancake syrup in a vintage cow-shaped creamer.

Bertie's Pecan Rolls

Roberta Scheeler
Ashley, OH

Turn a convenience product into a treat with homemade flavor!
Any leftover rolls can be reheated in the microwave for
20 seconds...they'll taste like they came right out of the oven.

1/4 c. butter, melted
1/4 c. maple syrup
1/2 c. chopped pecans

2 12.4-oz. tubes refrigerated
cinnamon rolls

In a small bowl, mix together butter, syrup and pecans. Spoon mixture equally into 12 greased muffin cups. Separate cinnamon rolls and cut into quarters; set aside the frosting from rolls. Place 4 quarters into each muffin cup, pressing together lightly. Bake at 350 degrees for 15 to 18 minutes. Invert rolls onto a serving platter. If desired, drizzle with reserved frosting. Serve warm. Makes one dozen.

Nothing is quite as intoxicating as the smell of bacon frying in the morning, save perhaps the smell of coffee brewing.

-James Beard

Quick Jam Danishes

Lisa Ashton
Aston, PA

You'll love these easy-to-make breakfast treats. They're yummy with strawberry, apricot or peach jam...you could even make a batch with several different flavors of jam!

8-oz. tube refrigerated crescent rolls
8 t. cream cheese, softened and divided

8 t. favorite-flavor jam, divided
Garnish: coarse sugar

Unroll crescent roll dough and separate into triangles. Place one teaspoon cream cheese on the long side of each triangle, mashing lightly; top the cream cheese with one teaspoon jam. Roll up triangle, starting with the long side, to secure cream cheese and jam inside. Pull over the point, pinching sides to seal. Place on an ungreased baking sheet; sprinkle with sugar. Bake at 375 degrees for 18 to 20 minutes, until golden. Makes 8.

Keep shopping simple...have a shopping list that includes all ingredients you normally use, plus a few blank lines for special items.

Busy-Day Breakfasts

Strawberry French Toast

Rosemary Zins
Alexandria, MN

Such a treat...perfect for a weekend brunch.

3 eggs, beaten
3/4 c. half-and-half
1 T. strawberry jam
8 thick slices French bread,
   halved diagonally

2 to 3 T. butter
Garnish: sliced strawberries,
   powdered sugar

In a shallow bowl, whisk together eggs, half-and-half and jam. Dip bread into mixture. Melt butter in a skillet over medium heat; cook bread on both sides until golden. Serve toast topped with a large dollop of Strawberry Butter, sliced strawberries and a dusting of powdered sugar. Makes 3 to 4 servings.

Strawberry Butter:

1/3 c. strawberry jam

1/4 c. butter, softened

Beat jam and butter with an electric mixer on low speed until well blended. Serve at room temperature.

Need some softened butter in a hurry? Grate chilled sticks of butter with a cheese grater...it will soften in just minutes!

Golden Waffles 1-2-3

Kathy Grashoff
Fort Wayne, IN

A simple recipe that comes together in no time at all!

8-oz. container fruit yogurt
2 eggs
3 T. oil

1 c. biscuit baking mix
1/4 c. cornmeal
Garnish: butter, maple syrup

In a bowl, combine yogurt, eggs and oil. Beat with an electric mixer on medium speed until smooth. Stir in baking mix and cornmeal. Ladle out 1/3 of batter into an oiled waffle iron. Bake according to manufacturer's instructions. Serve with butter and syrup. Makes 3 waffles.

While the waffles are baking, stir up a super-simple
fruit topping. Combine a can of fruit pie filling and
2 tablespoons orange or apple juice in a bowl. Microwave
for 2 to 2-1/2 minutes, stirring twice. Scrumptious!

Busy-Day Breakfasts

Scrambled Pancakes

Julie Larsen
Rutland, IA

Way back in elementary school, a close friend shared this recipe with me. It has been a favorite breakfast food for many years...I still think of my friend whenever I make these pancakes.

1 c. all-purpose flour
1/4 c. sugar
1/2 t. baking powder
1 c. milk

2 eggs, separated
2 T. butter
Garnish: maple syrup

In a bowl, mix together flour, sugar, baking powder, milk and egg yolks; set aside. In a separate bowl, with an electric mixer on high speed, beat egg whites until stiff. Gently fold in flour mixture. Melt butter in a 10" skillet and pour in all the batter. Cook over medium-low heat while continuously folding over. Cook until golden. Serve warm with syrup. Serves 4.

A healthy quick breakfast! Layer crunchy whole-grain cereal, fresh berries and creamy low-fat yogurt in a parfait cup. Add a spoon and breakfast is served! You can even snap on a lid and take it with you.

Apple Gem Cakes

Lorrie Smith
Drummonds, TN

This tasty recipe for fruit muffins came from my Grandmother Agnes.
She always called muffins by the old-fashioned name of "gem cakes."

2 c. self-rising flour
1/2 c. sugar
1 c. apple, cored, peeled and
   finely chopped
1 egg, beaten
1 c. milk

3 T. butter, melted and slightly
   cooled
1/3 c. brown sugar, packed
1/2 c. chopped pecans or
   walnuts
1/2 t. cinnamon

Sift flour and sugar together into a bowl. Add apple; mix well. In a
separate bowl, combine egg, milk and butter. Add to flour mixture
and stir just enough to moisten. Spoon into muffin cups that have
been sprayed with non-stick vegetable spray, filling 3/4 full. Combine
remaining ingredients; sprinkle over batter. Bake at 400 degrees for
15 to 20 minutes. Makes one dozen.

A thoughtful gesture that's ready in a snap! Make a new
neighbor feel welcome by giving her a wicker basket of
homebaked muffins, wrapped in a pretty napkin.

Busy-Day Breakfasts

Apple Pie Oatmeal

Jill Ball
Highland, UT

This is an easy, healthy and hearty breakfast that I serve often to my family...they love it!

1 c. water
1/2 c. long-cooking oats,
  uncooked
1/8 t. salt
2 t. brown sugar, packed

1 T. apple, cored, peeled
  and diced
1/8 t. apple pie spice
Garnish: milk or cream

Combine water, oats and salt in a microwave-safe bowl. Cover tightly with plastic wrap, folding back a small edge to allow steam to escape. Microwave on high for 2-1/2 minutes. Stir well. Top servings with remaining ingredients. Serves one.

For fuss-free mornings, hang up a country-style peg rack by the back door...you'll always know where to find the kids' backpacks, umbrellas and even the dog's leash!

Snappy Apple-Cinnamon Pizza

Abby Bills
Orleans, NE

When I made this sweet dessert-style pizza for our church's open house, it was a hit! It only takes minutes to put together too.

12.4-oz. tube refrigerated
   cinnamon rolls
21-oz. can apple pie filling

1/4 c. brown sugar, packed
1 T. butter, melted

Separate cinnamon rolls, setting aside the frosting from tube. Flatten each roll into a 4-inch circle. Arrange rolls on a greased 12" round pizza pan, overlapping edges to form a crust. Bake at 400 degrees for 8 minutes. Spoon pie filling over crust to within 1/2 inch of edge. Combine brown sugar and butter; sprinkle over pie filling. Bake an additional 6 to 8 minutes, or until crust is golden; cool. Warm reserved frosting slightly and drizzle over pizza; cut into wedges. Makes 10 to 12 servings.

COME INTO MY KITCHEN AND CHAT WITH ME WHILE I PREPARE A POT OF TEA.

Sending out invitations to brunch? Slip a spiced teabag into each envelope for a sweet surprise.

Quick Bites

Pizza-Style Nachos

*Lisa Ann Panzino DiNunzio
Vineland, NJ*

A yummy warm snack...guests of all ages can't resist it!

18-oz. pkg. tortilla chips
12-oz. jar pizza sauce
2 to 3 T. grated Parmesan
   cheese

salt and pepper to taste
8-oz. pkg. shredded mozzarella
   cheese

Spray a 15"x10" jelly-roll pan with non-stick vegetable spray. Spread tortilla chips evenly on pan. Spoon sauce lightly over chips, but don't saturate them. Sprinkle with Parmesan cheese, salt and pepper. Top with mozzarella cheese. Bake at 375 degrees for 10 to 15 minutes, until cheese is melted. Serve warm. Serves 6.

Show your hometown spirit...cheer on the high school football team with a neighborhood block party. Invite neighbors to bring along their favorite appetizers to share and don't forget to wear school colors!

Pretzels with an Attitude

Beckie Apple
Grannis, AR

Our family loves to watch sports on television...football, basketball, baseball...we love them all! These spicy pretzels are one of our favorite game-time or anytime snacks.

24-oz. pkg. mini twist pretzels
1-1/4 c. oil
2 T. red pepper flakes

2 T. ranch salad dressing mix
2 T. grated Parmesan cheese
2 t. Italian seasoning

Transfer pretzels to a one-gallon container with a tight-fitting lid. Shake to settle. Combine remaining ingredients in a bowl. Whisk until well mixed and pour over pretzels. Put lid on container and rotate until well coated, about 2 to 3 minutes. Let stand overnight before serving...if you can wait that long! Makes 20 to 24 servings.

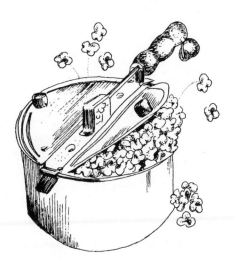

For a quick & easy snack that everybody loves, nothing beats a big bowl of fresh-popped popcorn! To add new flavor, sprinkle on grated Parmesan cheese, taco seasoning mix or cinnamon-sugar.

English Muffin Pizzas

Lilly Badeau
Manchester, NH

We all love these little mini pizzas...they're ready to eat in a jiffy!
Add pepperoni slices or other favorite toppings, if you like.

4 English muffins, split
1/2 c. pizza sauce

8-oz. pkg. shredded mozzarella
cheese

Place muffins on an ungreased baking sheet, split-side up. Spoon pizza sauce evenly over muffins; top with cheese. Bake at 375 degrees for 10 minutes, or until cheese is melted. Serves 4.

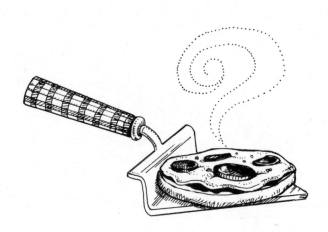

Set out all the fixin's for mini pizzas. Let the kids choose their favorite toppers, then pop the pizzas in the oven...a fun family meal or a festive sleep-over treat.

Quick **Bites**

Lake Charles Dip

Brenda Hughes
Houston, TX

This tasty dip recipe comes from my good friend, Candy. I was visiting her years ago and she served me this dip...I loved it so much that she gave me the recipe. It's named for Lake Charles, Louisiana where spicy food is always appreciated...it's a Cajun thing!

1 roma tomato, chopped
1 avocado, pitted, peeled and
   chopped
1 c. sour cream
1 T. mayonnaise

0.7-oz. pkg. Italian salad
   dressing mix
3 T. lemon juice
1/2 to 3/4 t. hot pepper sauce
tortilla chips

Combine all ingredients except tortilla chips; stir until blended. Cover and refrigerate for one hour before serving. Serve with tortilla chips. Makes 8 to 12 servings.

Homemade Tortilla Chips

Megan Brooks
Antioch, TN

Almost as easy as opening a bag of chips...and just two ingredients!
Serve with salsa or guacamole. Yummy!

6 corn tortillas, each cut into
   8 wedges

kosher salt to taste

Spread tortilla wedges on an ungreased baking sheet in a single layer. Bake at 350 degrees for 8 to 10 minutes, until crisp. While still warm, spray each chip lightly with non-stick vegetable spray. Sprinkle salt lightly over both sides of chips. Makes 4 dozen.

One of the delights of life is eating with friends.
-Laurie Colwin

Heavenly Warm Corn Dip

Allison Paschal
Royal, AR

My pastor's wife makes this zesty dip for every church potluck and there is never enough of it...it disappears that fast! Serve it with scoop-type corn chips to enjoy every bit.

8-oz. pkg. cream cheese,
  softened
10-oz. can diced tomatoes with
  chiles, drained
15-1/4 oz. can yellow corn,
  drained

15-oz. can shoepeg corn,
  drained
2 t. ground cumin
2 t. chili powder
1 t. garlic powder
salt to taste

Mix all ingredients together in a microwave-safe bowl. Microwave on high until heated through and cheese is melted, 2 to 3 minutes. Stir to blend; serve warm. Makes 8 to 12 servings.

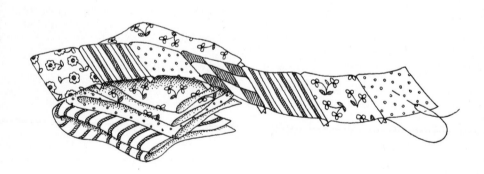

A table runner really dresses up a table, and you can make one in no time at all. Just stitch together several vintage-style tea towels, end-to-end.

Julie's Fresh Guacamole

Julie Dos Santos
Fort Pierce, FL

I love guacamole! I like it to be creamy and a little chunky, all at the same time. This recipe is much more delicious than store-bought guacamole, and it's so simple to make.

6 avocados, halved and pitted
3 T. lime juice
1/2 yellow onion, finely chopped
4 roma tomatoes, chopped
3/4 c. sour cream
1 T. ranch salad dressing
1 T. salt, or to taste
1 T. pepper, or to taste
1 T. chili powder
1/2 t. cayenne pepper
Garnish: fresh cilantro sprigs
tortilla chips

Scoop out avocado pulp into a large bowl; mash with a fork. Add lime juice, onion and tomatoes; mix with a spoon. Add sour cream, salad dressing and seasonings; mix well. Cover with plastic wrap; refrigerate for at least 30 minutes. Garnish with cilantro. Serve with tortilla chips. Makes 8 to 10 servings.

Grow a windowsill garden...fun for kids! Fill an empty jar with water, then use toothpicks to suspend a fresh avocado pit in the water. Place the jar in a sunny window...the new plant will form roots and leaves in just a few days.

Great-Aunt Laura's Cheese

Kate Kelly Gallegos
Aurora, IL

In our family, this recipe is legendary! We love it so much, we eat it out of the bowl with a spoon, but it's delicious as a dip with any kind of chips. We always double it because everyone wants a huge bowl for themselves...it's really that good!

16-oz. container cottage cheese
8-oz. container sour cream
3-oz. pkg. cream cheese,
   softened

2 T. milk
1 clove garlic, pressed
salt to taste

Combine all ingredients together in a large bowl. Beat with an electric mixer on low speed until smooth. Serves 4 to 8.

Parmesan Cheesy Twists

Rhonda Reeder
Ellicott City, MD

Buttery good, oh-so tasty, quick & easy!

2 eggs, beaten
2 T. water
1/2 c. grated Parmesan cheese
2 T. fresh parsley, chopped

1 t. dried oregano
17.3-oz. pkg. frozen puff pastry
   sheets, thawed

Whisk eggs and water together. In a separate bowl, combine cheese and herbs; set aside. Unfold one pastry sheet on a lightly floured surface. Roll out into a 14-inch by 10-inch rectangle; cut in half lengthwise. Brush one piece with half of egg mixture; sprinkle with half of cheese mixture. Top with the other piece, egg-side down. Cut into 1/2-inch wide strips; twist strips and place on a lightly greased baking sheet. Repeat with second pastry sheet. Bake at 400 degrees for 10 to 12 minutes, until golden. Makes 5 dozen.

BBQ Nachos Deluxe

Donna Roe
Merrimack, NH

My husband and I really enjoy these hearty nachos! He loves it because of the BBQ sauce and I love it because it's so easy.

1-1/2 lbs. ground beef
16-oz. can refried beans
18-oz. bottle barbecue sauce
20-oz. pkg. tortilla chips
2-1/4 oz. can sliced black olives,
   drained

2 8-oz. pkgs. shredded
   Mexican-blend cheese
Garnish: sour cream

Brown beef in a skillet over medium heat; drain. Stir in beans and barbecue sauce. Simmer until heated through, about 5 minutes. Spread tortilla chips evenly on an ungreased baking sheet. Spoon beef mixture evenly over chips. Sprinkle olives and cheese on top. Bake at 350 degrees for 15 to 18 minutes. Garnish with sour cream. Makes 4 to 6 servings.

Arrange nachos on a large oven-proof serving tray before popping them into the oven...one less pan to wash after the party!

Zesty Oyster Crackers

Michelle Lashbrook
Evansville, IN

*Kids and adults both love these flavorful crackers. My mom
used to make them for us to snack on after school...such a tasty
change from potato chips!*

2 12-oz. pkgs. oyster crackers
1 c. canola oil
1-oz. pkg. ranch salad dressing
  mix

1 t. dill weed
1/2 t. garlic powder

Place crackers in a large bowl; set aside. Mix together remaining
ingredients. Pour oil mixture over crackers and mix well. Store in large
plastic zipping bags. Serves 10.

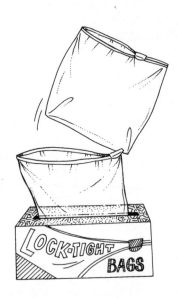

Lunch and after-school snacks
in a flash! Fill small plastic
zipping bags with individual
portions of a favorite snack.
Place all the little bags into
one big container...all ready
for treats as they're needed.

Quick Bites

Parmesan-Onion Canapés

Cora Wilfinger
Manitowoc, WI

An easy, tasty and inexpensive appetizer everyone will love. I've used this recipe for over twenty-five years, so you know it's tried & true. These go quickly, so be sure to save some for yourself!

1 loaf sliced party rye bread
1 c. mayonnaise
1 c. grated Parmesan cheese

1/2 c. onion, finely chopped
1 T. milk

Arrange rye slices in a single layer on a lightly greased baking sheet. Lightly toast under broiler, 4 inches from heat; remove from oven. In a bowl, combine remaining ingredients; stir until smooth. Spread mayonnaise mixture on each slice. Return to broiler for 2 minutes, until golden. Serves 10 to 12.

Appetizer spreads are perfect for enjoying during card games or a favorite movie at home with friends! Set out a variety of creamy dips, crunchy snacks and sweet munchies along with fizzy beverages...then relax and enjoy your guests.

Cheesy Chicken Quesadillas

Gretchen Brown
Forest Grove, OR

What's not to love about bacon, ranch dressing, chicken and cheese all melted together with a crispy tortilla? I created this recipe because it's a combination that my son likes. I can fix this quickly for him when he gets home late from after-school activities.

8 8-inch flour tortillas, divided
1/2 c. ranch salad dressing
1 c. shredded Monterey Jack
   cheese
1 c. shredded Cheddar cheese
12-1/2 oz. can chicken, drained
1/3 c. bacon bits
Garnish: salsa

Spread 4 tortillas evenly with salad dressing. Layer with cheeses, chicken, bacon and remaining tortillas. Place each quesadilla into a skillet sprayed with non-stick vegetable spray. Grill over medium-high heat for about 2 minutes on each side, until golden and cheese is melted. Let stand for 2 minutes; cut into wedges. Serve with salsa. Serves 4.

Make your pizza cutter do double duty...it's oh-so handy for slicing cheesy quesadillas into wedges too.

Quick ◇◇◇◇◇◇◇◇
Bites
◇◇◇◇◇◇◇◇◇◇

Sausage & Cheese Bites

Wanda Boykin
Lewisburg, TN

A friend at my church gave me this recipe. These hot sausage-topped bread slices are easy, quick & delicious.

1 lb. ground pork sausage
32-oz. pkg. pasteurized process
   cheese spread, cubed

1 loaf sliced party pumpernickel

Brown sausage in a skillet over medium heat; drain. Place cheese in a large microwave-safe container. Microwave on high for about 5 minutes until melted, stirring halfway through. Stir sausage into cheese. Spread cheese mixture on pumpernickel slices by tablespoonfuls. Place slices on ungreased baking sheets. Bake at 350 degrees for 10 minutes, until lightly golden. Serves 10 to 12.

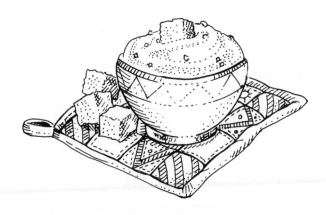

For an instant appetizer, toss a drained jar of Italian antipasto mix with bite-size cubes of mozzarella cheese. Serve with party picks.

Can't-Miss Creamy Beef Dip

Jean Cerutti
Kittanning, PA

Everyone will beg you for this recipe...it's a yummy,
fast alternative to the traditional cheese ball.

2 8-oz. pkgs. cream cheese, softened
8-oz. container spreadable Cheddar cheese
8-oz. pkg. shredded Cheddar cheese
1 bunch green onions, finely chopped
5-oz. jar dried beef, finely chopped
2 T. Worcestershire sauce
assorted crackers or chips

Blend cheeses together in a bowl. Add onions, beef and sauce; mix well. Cover and refrigerate at least 2 hours. Serve with crackers or chips. Serves 15 to 20.

Perfect Pita Chips

Tonya Sheppard
Galveston, TX

Bake up your own crisp chips in your favorite pita flavors.

12 pita bread rounds, split
1/2 c. olive oil
1/2 t. pepper
1 t. garlic salt

Cut each split pita round into 8 wedges. Arrange in a single layer on aluminum foil-lined baking sheets. Combine remaining ingredients in a small bowl. Brush mixture over both sides of each pita wedge. Bake at 400 degrees for 7 to 8 minutes, until crisp and lightly golden. Makes 8 dozen.

For the easiest-ever snack mix, toss together equal amounts of sweetened dried cranberries, salted peanuts and chocolate chips.

Zesty Chili Dip

Rosalyn Smith
Apache Junction, AZ

My husband shared this dip recipe with me at our first camping experience as a new family. It's speedy to make and hearty enough to be a meal. I'm sure you will like it too!

1 lb. ground beef
16-oz. pkg. Mexican pasteurized
   process cheese spread, cubed
15-oz. can hot chili with beans
15-oz. can chili with no beans
tortilla chips

Brown beef in a skillet over medium heat; drain. Add cheese and chili to skillet; reduce heat. Simmer for about 10 minutes, stirring occasionally, until cheese is melted. Serve warm with tortilla chips. Serves 5 to 10.

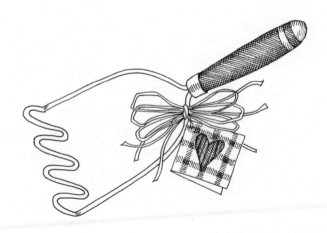

An easy way to crumble ground beef...use a potato masher. It makes browning so quick & easy.

Ham & Olive Roll-Ups

Lisa Herold
Abilene, TX

*This is a yummy snack for anyone on the go! A neighbor
gave me this recipe during the holidays.*

1 lb. deli sliced ham
2 8-oz. pkgs. cream cheese,
  softened

Optional: 1 T. pimentos, minced
4-1/2 oz. can whole black
  olives, drained

Pat ham slices dry with a paper towel. Spread cream cheese over one
side of each ham slice. Sprinkle with pimentos, if desired. Roll up ham
slice jelly-roll style; slice into one-inch thick pieces. Fasten each roll
with a toothpick topped with an olive. Serve immediately or refrigerate
until serving time. Serves 4 to 6.

Turn your favorite shredded pork, beef or chicken barbecue
recipe into a delicious appetizer. Serve up bite-size
sandwiches using brown & serve rolls as buns.

Quick Bites

Creamy Spinach Spirals

Marilyn Miller
Fort Washington, PA

This scrumptious appetizer recipe was handed down from my grandmother. It's oh-so easy to put together and everybody likes it!

2 10-oz. pkgs. frozen spinach, thawed and drained	1 c. sour cream
1 c. mayonnaise	4-oz. pkg. bacon bits
	12 10-inch flour tortillas

Combine all ingredients except tortillas; blend well. Spread a light layer of mixture over one side of each tortilla. Roll up tortillas jelly-roll style; slice into one-inch thick pieces. Cover and chill until ready to serve. Serves 10 to 12.

Ready-set-go snacks! When you need a little something extra for guests, but time is short, just pick up a few nibblers at the store. Assorted olives, fancy nuts, cream cheese and crackers, cubed cheese and shrimp cocktail all make quick & easy treats.

Terry's Hurricane Dill Dip

Teresa Rawnick
Palm Bay, FL

In 1995, when we were in the eye of Hurricane Erin, my best friend & next-door neighbor Traci called to ask if there was take-out for my homemade dill dip, calling it "Terry's Hurricane Dill Dip." She was kidding, of course, but it was so quick & easy that I whipped up a batch and ran it next door before the winds picked up again. We've called it Terry's Hurricane Dill Dip ever since!

1 c. plain yogurt
1 c. mayonnaise
1 T. dill weed
1 T. dried, minced onion

1/2 t. seasoned salt
potato chips, assorted cut-up
  vegetables

Combine all ingredients except potato chips and vegetables; mix thoroughly. Cover and chill for about one hour to blend flavors. Serve with your favorite chips or cut-up fresh vegetables. Makes 2 cups.

Dip to go! Spoon some creamy vegetable dip into a tall plastic cup and add crunchy celery and carrot sticks. Add a lid and the snack is ready to tote. Be sure to keep it chilled.

Quick Bites

Yummy Onion Dip

Linda Kehl
Attica, NY

*We enjoy this dip at our monthly card club. It's a hit
each time I make it!*

1 c. mayonnaise
1 c. shredded extra-sharp
  Cheddar sheese

1 c. onion, chopped
assorted crackers, tortilla chips,
  celery sticks

Mix mayonnaise, cheese and onion. Spread in a greased shallow
8"x8" baking pan. Bake, uncovered, at 350 degrees for 20 minutes, or
until bubbly and golden around the edges. Serve warm with crackers,
tortilla chips or celery sticks. Makes 3 cups.

Fill up a big party tray with crisp fresh veggies for dipping
and snacking...calorie-counting friends will thank you!
Any extras can be tossed into a crunchy salad the next day.

Sweet & Salty Party Mix

Coralita Truax
Perrysville, OH

*I've had this recipe for many years...this crunchy snack mix
is still a family favorite!*

2 c. bite-size crispy corn cereal
  squares
2 c. mini pretzel twists
1 c. dry-roasted peanuts

20 caramels, unwrapped and
  coarsely chopped
12-oz. pkg. white chocolate
  chips

In a large bowl, combine all ingredients except chocolate chips. Toss
to mix and set aside. Place chocolate chips in a microwave-safe
container. Microwave on high until melted, one to 2 minutes; stir
until smooth. Pour over cereal mixture; toss to coat. Immediately
spread onto a wax paper-lined baking sheet; let stand until set,
about 20 minutes. Break into pieces. Store in an airtight container.
Serves 4 to 6.

Clever party favors in a jiffy! Spoon party mix into empty
cardboard tubes. Wrap each tube in colorful tissue paper
and secure the open ends with curling ribbon...all ready
for guests to take home.

Crunching Zoo Mix

Shirl Parsons
Cape Carteret, NC

*Kids love this crunchy fun-to-eat mix! If desired, replace the peanuts
with dried banana chips or fruit bits...even add fish- or
bear-shaped crackers as you like.*

2 c. animal crackers
2 c. chocolate-covered raisins

1 c. jellybeans
1 c. unsalted peanuts

Combine all ingredients in a large bowl; toss to mix. Store in an
airtight container or plastic zipping bag. Makes 6 cups.

A sunny day is perfect for a family adventure.
Pack the cooler with yummy snacks, load up the minivan
and head out for somewhere you've always wanted
to go...a state park, an outdoor museum or the zoo.
New memories in the making!

Caramel Cereal Mix Treat

Jennifer Seals
Quincy, IL

Once you start snacking on this, you can't stop! So quick & easy to make. Perfect for fall treat bags or tucking into lunchboxes.

12-oz. pkg. corn & rice cereal
16-oz. jar dry-roasted peanuts
3/4 c. butter

1-1/2 c. brown sugar, packed
1/2 c. corn syrup
1 t. baking soda

Combine cereal and peanuts in a large microwave-safe bowl; set aside. In a heavy saucepan over medium heat, combine butter, brown sugar and corn syrup. Cook until butter melts; bring to a gentle boil, stirring frequently. Boil for 2 minutes. Remove saucepan from heat and stir in baking soda. Pour butter mixture over cereal mixture; stir to coat. Microwave on high for 6 minutes, stirring every 2 minutes until cereal is well coated. Pour onto lightly greased baking sheets. Cool; break apart and store in an airtight container. Makes about 17 cups.

Paper cupcake liners come in all colors...great for serving single portions of chips or party mix!

Brown Sugar Fruit Dip

Kathy Harris
Valley Center, KS

When I need a quick & easy appetizer, this dip is always a winner.
My favorite fruits for dipping are strawberries, grapes, apple wedges
and pineapple spears. Gingersnaps are tasty too.

8-oz. pkg. cream cheese,
   softened
1/2 c. brown sugar, packed
1 c. sour cream
1 t. vanilla extract

1 c. frozen whipped topping,
   thawed
assorted fruit slices, gingersnap
   cookies

Combine cream cheese and brown sugar in a bowl. Beat with an
electric mixer on medium speed until smooth. Add sour cream and
vanilla; beat until blended and smooth. Fold in whipped topping.
Cover and chill for at least 4 hours before serving. Serve with fruit or
gingersnaps. Makes 8 to 10 servings.

Vintage paper road maps make fun table
coverings...unusual conversation starters too! Pick them up
for pennies at a thrift store or used bookstore. Cover them
with clear plastic, or just toss 'em away afterwards.

Crunchy No-Bake Squares

Carol Hickman
Kingsport, TN

These irresistible candy-filled squares make a great snack to take along on road trips...that is, if they don't all get eaten up first!

1 c. corn syrup
1 c. sugar
12-oz. jar creamy peanut butter

6 c. corn flake cereal
1 c. candy-coated chocolate
  mini-baking bits

In a Dutch oven over medium-high heat, bring corn syrup and sugar to a rolling boil. Remove from heat; stir in peanut butter until smooth. Add cereal and baking bits, stirring gently to combine. Spread into a greased 13"x9" baking pan. Cool and cut into squares. Makes 2 dozen.

Need a quick after-school snack for the kids that's a change from the same old PB & J? Spread peanut butter and strawberry jam on pita rounds, then top with peanuts and sliced strawberries...yum!

Chocolate Pinwheels

Lisa Ashton
Aston, PA

*One night my kids were asking for a quick
treat...this was the tasty result!*

11-oz. tube refrigerated bread
    sticks
3/4 c. semi-sweet chocolate
    chips

1/4 c. butter, melted
1/2 c. sugar

Unroll bread sticks and cut them in half. Press chocolate chips in
a single row along the top of each bread stick half; roll up into a
pinwheel. Arrange pinwheels on a parchment paper-lined baking sheet.
Brush with melted butter; sprinkle with sugar. Bake at 350 degrees for
10 to 12 minutes, until golden. Makes 16.

Part of the secret of success in life is to eat
what you like and let the food fight it out inside.
-Mark Twain

Pink Lassies

Susan Maurer
Dahlgren, IL

*When I was growing up, I used to request this fruity beverage often.
It's still delightful and makes a refreshing summertime treat.*

1 c. cranberry juice cocktail
1/4 c. orange juice

1 c. vanilla ice cream

Combine all ingredients in a blender. Cover and blend until smooth.
Serve in tall glasses with straws. Makes 2 servings.

New plastic sand pails make whimsical servers for chips and
snacks. They're inexpensive, come in lots of bright colors
and, perhaps best of all, stack easily so storage is a snap.

Quick Bites

Famous Moo Moo-Shake

McKenzie Thomason
Mountain Home, ID

I'm eleven years old and I like to create recipes. I have a dream of being a famous chef someday and having my own TV show. For a variation, I suggest using strawberry ice cream and adding a cup of strawberries...yummy!

2 c. milk
1 scoop vanilla ice cream
1 scoop chocolate ice cream

3 T. chocolate syrup
Optional: crushed ice

Combine all ingredients in a blender; blend until smooth. Serve over ice, if desired. Makes 2 servings.

A photo album is just right for keeping frequently-used recipes handy on the kitchen counter. Tuck in a few photos of happy family mealtimes too!

Reuben Dip

Linda Sickler
Brush Prairie, WA

This is my most-requested appetizer at gatherings and believe me, there are never any leftovers!

1/2 lb. deli corned beef, diced
8-oz. pkg. cream cheese,
   softened
1 c. shredded Swiss cheese
1 c. sauerkraut, drained

1/2 c. sour cream
1 T. catsup
2 t. spicy brown mustard
rye crackers or sliced party
   rye bread

Stir all ingredients except crackers or bread together in a bowl; spoon into a greased one-quart casserole dish. Bake, uncovered, at 350 degrees for 30 minutes, or until hot and bubbly. Serve warm with rye crackers or party rye slices. Makes 4 cups.

Hot Crackers

Scooter Pugh
El Dorado, AR

An oldie but goodie with a peppery new taste...perfect for munching!

16-oz. pkg. saltine crackers
1 T. red pepper flakes
1-oz. pkg. dry ranch salad
   dressing mix

1/2 t. garlic powder
1-1/3 c. canola oil

Place crackers in a gallon glass jar with a tight-fitting lid. Mix together remaining ingredients and pour over crackers. Turn jar on its side; roll until crackers are well coated. Let stand 2 to 3 hours, then break apart and store in an airtight container. Makes about one pound.

No-Fuss Soups & Sandwiches

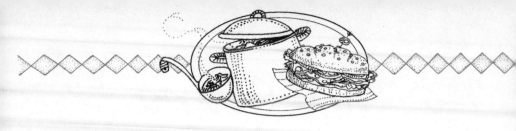

Hot & Tasty Hoagies

Jo Ann

*Hoagies, poorboys, grinders, submarine sandwiches...whatever you
call 'em, at our house we love 'em! Use any combination
of deli meats and cheeses you like.*

6 6-inch hoagie rolls, split
1/2 c. Italian salad dressing
1/2 lb. deli ham, sliced
1/2 lb. deli salami, sliced
1/2 lb. deli capicola, sliced

8-oz. pkg. provolone cheese
   slices
1 to 2 tomatoes, thinly sliced
1/2 onion, thinly sliced
Optional: pepperoncini

Brush both cut sides of each roll with salad dressing. Layer bottom
halves of rolls evenly with meats and cheese. Top with tomato, onion
and pepperoncini, if desired. Replace tops of rolls; wrap rolls in
aluminum foil. Bake at 375 degrees for 12 to 15 minutes. Carefully
remove foil before serving. Makes 6 sandwiches.

Fill up a relish tray with crunchy fresh cut-up veggies
as a simple side dish for sandwiches. A creamy salad
dressing can even do double duty as a veggie dip
and a sandwich spread.

Rapid Reubens

Deb Blean
Morrison, IL

Add some crisp dill pickles and crinkled potato chips...dinner is served!

12-oz. can corned beef, chopped
14-oz. pkg. sauerkraut, drained
8-oz. pkg. Swiss cheese slices

Thousand Island salad dressing
   to taste
8 slices rye bread, toasted

Place corned beef in a microwave-safe 2-quart casserole dish. Top with sauerkraut and cheese. Cover with plastic wrap. Microwave on high for one to 2 minutes, or until cheese melts. Spread salad dressing on bread as desired. Top 4 bread slices with corned beef mixture; close with remaining bread. Makes 4 sandwiches.

Stock the cupboard with cans of chicken, tuna, corned beef and other canned meats. They make it oh-so easy to toss together all kinds of tasty meals in a jiffy.

Cabbage Patch Soup

Amy Woods
Collinsville, TX

My mom used to make this soup whenever the weather turned snowy or icy. I even remember Dad heading into town with chains on his tires to pick up the ingredients! No snow day is complete without a pot of Cabbage Patch Soup bubbling on the stove...and it's so simple that Mom can enjoy the snow day too.

1 head cabbage, chopped
1 lb. ground beef, browned and
  drained
10-3/4 oz. can cream of
  mushroom soup
10-3/4 oz. can Cheddar cheese
  soup

10-oz. can diced tomatoes with
  green chiles
Optional: saltine crackers,
  Cheddar cheese slices

Place cabbage in a stockpot; add just enough water to cover. Bring water to a boil over medium-high heat. Reduce heat; cover and simmer until cabbage is tender, about 15 to 20 minutes. Stir in remaining ingredients except crackers and cheese. Simmer an additional 20 minutes. If desired, serve with crackers and cheese. Serves 6.

Put dinner on the to-do list and resist the urge to answer phone messages or read the mail. Focusing on the task at hand will help make a meal faster and easier too!

Triple-Take Grilled Cheese

Abigail Smith
Gooseberry Patch

Delicious in winter with a steaming bowl of tomato soup...scrumptious in summer made with produce fresh from the garden!

1 T. oil
8 slices sourdough bread
1/4 c. butter, softened and divided
4 slices white American cheese
4 slices Muenster cheese

1/4 c. shredded sharp Cheddar cheese
Optional: 4 slices red onion, 4 slices tomato, 1/4 c. chopped fresh basil

Heat oil in a skillet over medium heat. Spread 2 bread slices with one tablespoon butter; place one slice butter-side down on skillet. Layer one slice American, one slice Muenster and 2 tablespoons Cheddar cheese on bread. If desired, top with an onion slice, a tomato slice and one tablespoon basil. Butter another slice of bread; add to sandwich in skillet. Reduce heat to medium-low. Cook until golden on one side, about 3 to 5 minutes; flip and cook until golden on the other side. Repeat with remaining ingredients. Makes 4 sandwiches.

Let your countertop meat grill do double duty...it's terrific for grilling thick sandwiches to perfection.

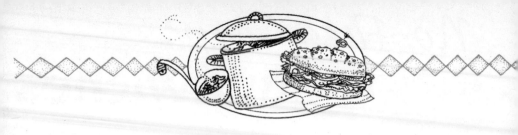

Tomato-Basil Bisque

Stephanie Mayer
Portsmouth, VA

Such an easy, yummy way to dress up a can of tomato soup!

10-oz. can fire-roasted diced
   tomatoes with garlic
10-3/4 oz. can tomato soup

1 c. milk
3 T. pesto sauce

Mix together all ingredients in a saucepan over medium-low heat.
Simmer until heated through. If desired, use an immersion blender to
purée soup to desired consistency. Serves 4.

Tomato-Spinach Soup

Lisa Langston
Montgomery, TX

I love tomatoes and spinach...what could be better than this?

10-3/4 oz. can tomato soup
1-1/3 c. milk
1 c. baby spinach

pepper to taste
Garnish: saltine crackers

In a saucepan over medium-low heat, combine tomato soup and milk.
Blend until smooth; add spinach. Simmer until heated through,
stirring frequently. Add pepper to taste. Serve with crackers. Serves 2.

Stir some alphabet pasta into a pot of
vegetable soup...you'll feel like a kid again!

Kielbasa Chowder

Jasmine Clifton
Colorado Springs, CO

I've been making this soup for several years and, without a doubt, it's my most-requested recipe. Everyone raves about it...try it and see if you don't agree!

1/4 c. butter
2 sweet onions, thinly sliced
salt and pepper to taste
1/8 t. allspice
2 potatoes, peeled and diced

3 c. chicken broth
1 qt. half-and-half
14-oz. pkg. frozen corn
14-oz. pkg. Kielbasa sausage, cut into bite-size pieces

Melt butter in a stockpot over medium-high heat. Stir in onions; sprinkle with seasonings. Cook until dark and caramelized, about 8 minutes, stirring frequently. Add potatoes and broth. Reduce heat; simmer until potatoes are tender, about 15 minutes. Add half-and-half and corn; heat through. Remove 3 cups soup to a blender; process on high setting and return to stockpot. Add sausage; heat through. Season with additional salt and pepper as needed. Makes 6 to 8 servings.

A soup supper in front of a crackling fire...how cozy!
Invite friends to bring their favorite veggies and cook up a
big pot of hearty soup together. While the soup simmers,
you can catch up on conversation.

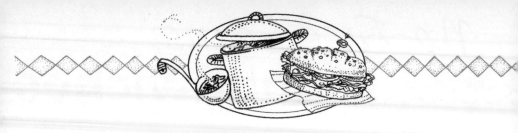

Cream of Broccoli Soup

Sharon Ninde
Geneva, IN

Equally good for a chilly-evening meal or a ladies' luncheon.

10-3/4 oz. can cream of potato
   soup
10-3/4 oz. can cream of chicken
   soup
1-3/4 c. milk

10-oz. pkg. frozen chopped
   broccoli, cooked and drained
1/8 t. onion powder
1/8 t. cayenne pepper
1/2 c. shredded Cheddar cheese

In a saucepan over medium heat, stir soups and milk together until smooth. Add broccoli and seasonings. Bring to a boil, stirring frequently. Reduce heat and simmer for 5 minutes. Add cheese and stir until melted. Serves 4.

Evaporated milk can be substituted whenever
a recipe calls for regular milk. Keep a few cans
on hand for rich, creamy soups.

Willy Strange's Good Soup

Jessica Branch
Colchester, IL

This recipe was given to me by my aunt. We were bored with chili...we tried this flavor-filled soup and it immediately became a favorite! Willy Strange was the name on the recipe and nobody knows why. We still laugh about it because it is such a funny name for a soup.

1 onion, diced
1 T. oil
1 lb. ground beef
2 10-3/4 oz. cans minestrone
   soup
10-3/4 oz. can tomato soup
15-oz. can ranch-style beans

10-oz. can diced tomatoes with
   green chiles
2 c. water
1/4 c. catsup
1/8 t. salt
1/8 t. pepper

In a Dutch oven over medium-high heat, sauté onion in oil. Add beef and brown; drain. Add remaining ingredients; bring to a boil. Reduce heat to low. Cover and simmer for about 30 minutes, or until soup thickens. Makes 8 servings.

Planning a busy-day soup supper? Let the slow cooker help out! In the morning, toss in all the ingredients and turn it to the low setting. A recipe that simmers for one to two hours on the stovetop can usually cook all day on low without overcooking.

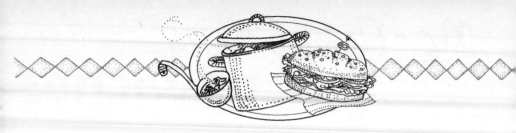

Bumsteads

Carol Mackley
Manheim, PA

*This is one of the Depression-era recipes my mother used to make.
They were simple and inexpensive, but we thought they were
really delicious...I bet you will too!*

3 eggs, hard-boiled, peeled and
chopped
1/4 lb. white American cheese,
diced
6-oz. can tuna, drained
2 T. green pepper, chopped

2 T. green olives with pimentos,
chopped
2 T. sweet pickle relish
1/2 c. mayonnaise
8 hot dog buns, split

Combine all ingredients except buns; spoon into buns. Arrange on
an aluminum foil-lined baking sheet. Bake at 350 degrees for 15 to
20 minutes, or until heated through and cheese is melted. Makes
8 sandwiches.

Use a potato peeler to quickly cut thin curls of cheese
for garnishing soup, salads or pasta.

Speedy Pizza Burgers

Emily Stiteler
Coshocton, OH

This recipe was a favorite meal for my husband when he was growing up, and now our kids love it too! It's incredibly delicious...puts a whole new spin on burgers!

1 lb. ground beef
14-1/2 oz. can diced tomatoes
  with garlic

8 hamburger buns, split
2 c. shredded mozzarella cheese

In a skillet over medium heat, brown beef; drain. Stir in tomatoes. Reduce heat and simmer for 3 minutes, stirring often. Remove from heat. Place bun bottoms on an aluminum foil-lined baking sheet; set aside tops. Spoon beef mixture onto bun bottoms. Sprinkle evenly with cheese; replace tops. Bake at 325 degrees for about 5 minutes, just until cheese is melted and buns are golden. Remove from oven; let stand for 2 minutes before serving. Makes 8 sandwiches.

A vintage-style oilcloth tablecloth with colorful fruit and flowers adds cheer to any dinner table. Its wipe-clean ease makes it oh-so practical for family meals.

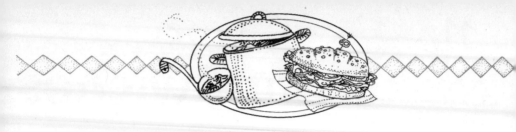

Tomato-Noodle Soup

Annette Varcoe
Brackney, PA

This is a recipe I found in my great-aunt's recipe box. She was a teenager during the Depression and knew how to stretch a penny into a dollar. I like to serve it with a tossed salad and garlic bread.

2 T. butter
1 T. all-purpose flour
4 c. tomato juice

1-1/2 c. water
1/4 c. sugar
2 c. thin egg noodles, uncooked

Melt butter in a heavy saucepan over medium heat; whisk in flour. Add tomato juice, water and sugar; whisk together. Bring to a low boil; add noodles. Cook for 10 minutes until noodles are tender, stirring occasionally. Remove from heat and cool for 10 minutes; stir again before serving. Serves 4.

Whip up some egg sandwiches for a tasty, super-quick meal. Scramble eggs as you like, tossing in shredded cheese or diced ham for extra flavor. Serve on toast alongside bowls of hot soup or fresh fruit cups...ready in a flash!

Avocado Egg Salad

Crystal Bruns
Iliff, CO

A fresh and delicious twist on egg salad...serve it on your favorite hearty bread!

6 eggs, hard-boiled, peeled and
   chopped
2 avocados, pitted, peeled and
   cubed
1/2 c. red onion, minced

3 T. sweet pickles, chopped
1 T. mustard
1/3 c. mayonnaise
salt and pepper to taste

Mash eggs with a fork in a bowl until crumbly. Add remaining ingredients except salt and pepper. Gently mix ingredients together until blended. Add salt and pepper to taste. Makes 6 servings.

Try this for perfect hard-boiled eggs every time! Cover eggs with water in a saucepan. Bring to a boil, then remove from heat, cover the pan and let stand for 18 to 20 minutes. Immediately plunge the eggs into ice water and peel.

Tailgating Taco Soup

Judy Pittenger
Richfield, WI

*A family favorite that I serve when we're watching football
on TV...it is easy, sooo good and always a hit!*

1 lb. ground beef chuck
1 onion, chopped
3 15-1/2 oz. cans Mexican-
   style chili beans
14-1/2 oz. can diced tomatoes
15-oz. can tomato sauce
4-1/2 oz. can diced green chiles

1-oz. pkg. ranch salad dressing
   mix
1-1/2 c. water
Garnish: shredded lettuce,
   chopped tomato, sour cream,
   shredded Cheddar cheese,
   corn chips

In a Dutch oven over medium-high heat, cook beef and onion until
beef is browned and onion is tender. Drain. Stir in remaining
ingredients except garnish; do not drain vegetables. Bring to a boil.
Reduce heat and simmer, uncovered, 15 minutes, stirring
occasionally. Spoon soup into bowls; garnish with desired toppings.
Makes 10 to 12 servings.

Whenever top-it-yourself tacos, sandwiches or soup are
on the menu, a muffin tin makes a terrific garnish server.
Fill each of the cups with something different...salsa,
sour cream, shredded cheese, diced tomatoes and any
other toppings. So easy to tote to the table!

Feel-Better BLT Sandwiches

Jen Chambers
Veneta, OR

My husband made these sandwiches for me when I had a bad cold and he stayed home to take care of me. They'll make anyone feel better in a hurry! For a real wake-you-up flavor, use creamy horseradish instead of the mayo and blue cheese.

8 slices whole-wheat bread,
  toasted
1 lb. thick-cut bacon, crisply
  cooked and crumbled

4 leaves Romaine lettuce
1 to 2 tomatoes, sliced
2 to 4 T. crumbled blue cheese
Garnish: mayonnaise, mustard

Layer 4 bread slices with bacon, lettuce and tomato slices. Sprinkle blue cheese over tomatoes. Spread mayonnaise and mustard on remaining 4 bread slices. Close sandwiches and serve. Makes 4 sandwiches.

Toast sandwich bread or buns before adding the fillings...it only takes a minute and makes such a tasty difference!

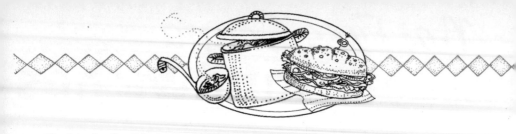

Special Chicken Noodle Soup

Bobbie Jockumsen
Idaho Falls, ID

Whenever I'm taking a meal to a neighbor who's sick or who has a new baby, I stir up this soup to give with a loaf of homemade bread. It's always much appreciated!

8 c. water
8 t. chicken bouillon granules
6-1/2 c. wide egg noodles,
  uncooked

2 10-3/4 oz. cans cream of
  chicken soup
3 c. cooked chicken, cubed
1 c. sour cream

In a stockpot over medium heat, bring water and bouillon to a boil. Add noodles and cook until tender, about 10 minutes. Do not drain! Stir in soup and chicken; heat through. Remove from heat and stir in sour cream. Serves 4 to 6.

Need to feed a few extra guests? It's easy to stretch soup! Some quick-cooking add-ins are instant rice, orzo pasta, ramen noodles and canned veggies. Simmer for just a few minutes, until tender.

Creamy Chicken Sandwiches

Karen Hazelett
Fort Wayne, IN

Growing up in the country, we kids always looked forward to church and town socials, where we could see our friends and eat some yummy homemade creamy chicken sandwiches. As we grew older, Mom would make these up and freeze portion sizes in muffin tins to send home with us as care packages!

27-oz. can chicken, drained
26-oz. can chicken broth
10-3/4 oz. can cream of chicken
   soup

1-1/4 c. saltine cracker crumbs
1 cube chicken bouillon
salt and pepper to taste
8 to 10 hamburger buns, split

Combine all ingredients except buns in a stockpot. Simmer over medium heat until thickened and heated through. If needed, add more cracker crumbs to thicken or water to thin. Serve on hamburger buns. Serves 8 to 10.

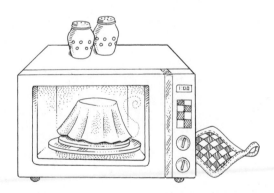

A dollar-store package of paper coffee filters is oh-so handy
in the kitchen. Use them as sandwich or taco holders,
fill them with chips or popcorn at snacktime...even lay
them over food being reheated in the microwave
to cut down on spattering.

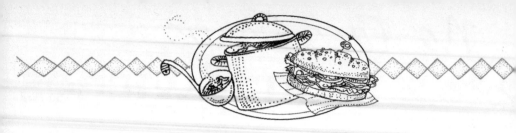

Egg Salad Sandwiches

Cherylann Smith
Efland, NC

Some days, there's nothing better than an old-fashioned egg salad sandwich and a cup of soup! Adjust the mayonnaise and mustard amounts to suit your family's taste.

1 doz. eggs, hard-boiled, peeled
   and chopped
1/2 c. mayonnaise
2 T. Dijon mustard
salt and pepper to taste

paprika to taste
1 loaf sliced whole-wheat bread,
   divided
Garnish: tomato slices

Mix together eggs, mayonnaise, mustard, salt and pepper until well blended. Sprinkle with paprika. Spoon onto half of bread slices. Top with tomato slices and remaining bread slices. Makes 10 to 12 servings.

Spoon homemade egg salad onto toasted sandwich buns, into hearty pita pockets or stuff inside a fresh-picked tomato...it's delicious no matter how it's served!

Chicken Dumpling Soup

Diana Chaney
Olathe, KS

My best friend from college gave me this recipe. I have been making it for over ten years. It's my favorite comfort food.

6 boneless chicken thighs
2 10-3/4 oz. cans cream of
   celery soup

salt and pepper to taste
12-oz. tube refrigerated biscuits,
   torn

Place chicken in a soup pot over high heat; add water to cover. Bring to a boil over high heat. Reduce heat to medium and simmer for 15 to 20 minutes, until chicken juices run clear. Drain, reserving 3 cups broth in the pot. Remove chicken and cool; shred chicken and return to broth. Stir in soup, salt and pepper; add biscuit pieces. Simmer over medium heat for 7 to 8 minutes, until dumplings are done. Serves 6.

Soups can be garnished with lots of tasty toppers...toasted nuts, crispy crumbled bacon, sour cream, croutons, snipped fresh parsley or shredded cheese. Try something new!

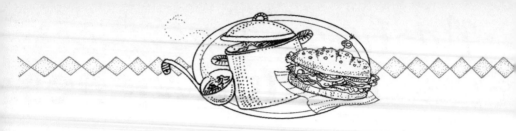

Mom's Turkey Burgers

Jenna Anderson
Tucson, AZ

Since I moved away from home, my mother's turkey burgers have become a comfort food for me...the yummy smell and taste take me right back home. Super fast...dinner in less than 15 minutes!

1 lb. ground turkey	2 T. mustard
1 onion, chopped	1 T. catsup
1 to 2 T. oil	1/2 t. salt
10-3/4 oz. can chicken gumbo soup	4 to 6 hamburger buns, split

In a skillet over medium heat, brown turkey and onion in oil; drain. Add remaining ingredients except buns. Mix together and cook until heated through. Serve on hamburger buns. Makes 4 to 6 servings.

Let the kids help make dinner! Younger children can set the table and tear lettuce for salad...older kids can measure, chop, stir and maybe even help with meal planning and shopping.

Southern Flair Soup

Kirstyn Kissam
Niceville, FL

This was the first real meal I cooked for my family...everyone loved it and now it's requested at least once a week! The ingredient list may look long but the soup goes together in a hurry.

1 lb. ground beef
1 onion, chopped
3 cloves garlic, minced
1-1/4 oz. pkg. taco seasoning
  mix
14-1/2 oz. can corn
14-1/2 oz. can pinto beans,
  drained and rinsed
14-1/2 oz. can black beans,
  drained and rinsed

6-oz. can chopped green chiles
2 14-1/2 oz. cans diced
  tomatoes
2 14-1/2 oz. cans chicken broth
juice of 3 limes
1/2 c. fresh cilantro, chopped
Garnish: shredded Mexican-
  blend cheese, sour cream,
  corn chips

In a stockpot over medium heat, brown beef with onion and garlic. Add taco seasoning; stir until well blended. Add corn, beans, chiles, tomatoes and broth. Bring to a boil; reduce heat to low, cover and simmer for 10 to 15 minutes. At serving time, stir in lime juice and cilantro. Ladle into bowls; garnish as desired. Serves 8 to 10.

If you like sweet cornbread, you'll love this family-size recipe! Mix together an 8-1/2 ounce box of corn muffin mix, a 9-ounce box of yellow cake mix, 1/2 cup water, 1/3 cup milk and 2 beaten eggs. Pour into a greased 13"x9" baking pan and bake at 350 degrees for 15 to 20 minutes. Scrumptious!

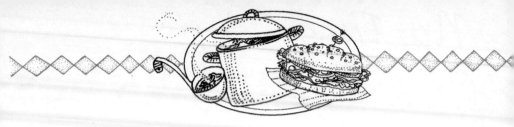

Caesar Focaccia Sandwich

Wendy Ball
Battle Creek, MI

Now that I'm retired after twenty-eight years of federal service,
I enjoy being able to try new recipes on my family. This one was
a big winner!

2 c. mixed salad greens
1/4 c. Caesar salad dressing
8-inch round focaccia bread,
   halved horizontally
4 slices Cheddar cheese
1/4 lb. deli ham, thinly shaved

1/4 lb. deli turkey, thinly shaved
1 tomato, sliced
1 slice red onion, separated
   into rings
Garnish: pickles, potato chips

Toss salad greens with salad dressing; set aside. Layer the bottom half
of focaccia with greens mixture and remaining ingredients except
garnish. Add the top half of focaccia; cut into halves or quarters.
Serve with pickles and chips on the side. Serves 2 to 4.

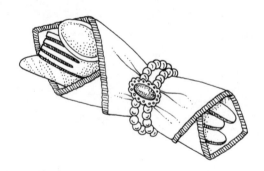

Real cloth napkins make mealtime just a little more
special...and they're a must when serving soup &
sandwiches! Stitch fun charms to napkin rings,
so everyone can identify their own napkin easily.

No-Fuss Soups
& Sandwiches

Cream of Fresh Vegetable Soup

Tonya Adams
Magnolia, KY

Homemade soup packed with five kinds of veggies...scrumptious!

3 potatoes, peeled and finely
   chopped
2 c. water
1/2 c. carrots, peeled and thinly
   sliced
1/2 c. green beans, trimmed
   and sliced
1/2 c. celery, chopped

1/2 c. peas
1/3 c. onion, sliced
3 c. milk
1/4 c. butter
1-3/4 t. salt
1/2 t. pepper

Cover potatoes with water in a large stockpot. Bring to a boil over medium-high heat; reduce heat and simmer until tender. Mash potatoes in saucepan; add remaining ingredients. Simmer until vegetables are tender and soup is heated through. Makes 5 servings.

For thick, creamy vegetable soup, use a hand-held immersion blender to purée some of the cooked veggies right in the stockpot.

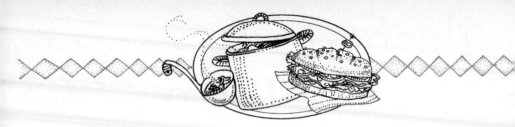

Carol's Beef Boats

Carol Jordan
Gilbert, AZ

I developed this sandwich recipe twenty years ago when my kids were young...it has stood the test of time! They are speedy to make, easy to take and can feed a crowd.

2 lbs. ground beef
1 onion, finely chopped
salt and pepper to taste
10-3/4 oz. can cream of
  mushroom soup

1 c. shredded Cheddar cheese
12 French rolls, split

Brown beef and onion in a large skillet over medium heat. Drain; add salt and pepper to taste. Add soup and heat through. Stir in cheese; cook until melted. Hollow out bottoms of rolls. Spoon beef mixture into rolls and replace tops. Wrap sandwiches individually in aluminum foil. Bake at 350 degrees for 15 minutes. Makes 12 sandwiches.

Fresh fruit salad is a scrumptious, healthy side that just about everyone will love. Cut two to three kinds of seasonal fruit into cubes and toss with a simple dressing made of equal parts honey and lemon or orange juice.

Beefy Noodle Soup

Mary Gage
Wakewood, CA

*A hearty stew-like soup...just add a basket of biscuits
and dinner is served.*

1 lb. stew beef, cubed
1/2 onion, chopped
1 to 2 T. oil
2 14-1/2 oz. cans Italian-style
   stewed tomatoes
2 10-1/2 oz. cans beef broth
16-oz. pkg. frozen mixed
   vegetables

1 t. dried oregano
1/2 t. salt
1/4 t. pepper
1 c. medium egg noodles,
   uncooked

In a Dutch oven over medium-high heat, brown beef and onion in oil; drain. Add remaining ingredients except noodles. Bring to a boil; stir in noodles. Reduce heat to medium-low; cover and cook for 10 to 15 minutes, until noodles are tender. Makes 6 to 8 servings.

Soups taste even better the next day...why not make a double batch? Let it cool thoroughly, then cover and refrigerate for up to 3 days. Supper tonight, an easy lunch later on.

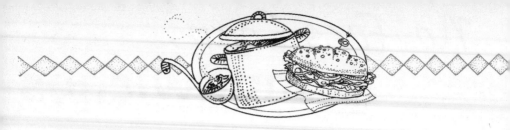

Pepper Steak Sammies

Vickie

Add your favorite steak sauce or seasoning salt...it's a great way to use leftover steak from last night's cookout too!

1 to 1-1/4 lbs. beef sirloin or
   ribeye steak
2 green peppers, thinly sliced
1 onion, sliced
4 cloves garlic, minced and
   divided

1 T. oil
salt and pepper to taste
1/3 c. butter, softened
4 French rolls, split and toasted

Grill or broil steak to desired doneness; set aside. In a skillet over medium heat, sauté green peppers, onion and half of garlic in oil until crisp-tender; drain. Slice steak thinly; add to skillet and heat through. Sprinkle with salt and pepper. Blend butter and remaining garlic; spread over cut sides of rolls. Spoon steak mixture onto bottom halves of rolls; add tops. Serves 4.

Keeping bottled minced garlic on hand saves time when you're in a hurry. When swapping it for fresh, remember that 1/2 teaspoon equals one clove.

No-Fuss Soups & Sandwiches

Hearty, Healthy Chicken Salad
Heather Cooper
Everett, WA

I first made this recipe one summer when I was craving a Thanksgiving leftovers sandwich and didn't want to roast a turkey. It turned out to be a big hit! I make it often now. All ingredients are to taste, so add more or less of anything to your liking.

4 boneless, skinless chicken
    breasts, cooked and diced
1/2 c. celery, chopped
1/4 c. onion, chopped
1/2 c. sweetened dried
    cranberries

1/4 c. sunflower kernels
1/2 to 1 c. low-fat plain yogurt
1-1/2 t. dried sage
1-1/2 t. poultry seasoning
10 slices favorite bread, toasted

In a large bowl, combine all ingredients except yogurt, seasonings and bread. Slowly stir in yogurt until ingredients are moistened to your preference. Add seasonings to taste. Serve on toasted bread. Makes about 5 sandwiches.

Whip up some cool, fruity coleslaw in a jiffy. Toss a bag of shredded coleslaw mix with mandarin orange segments or pineapple tidbits and just enough bottled coleslaw dressing to moisten.

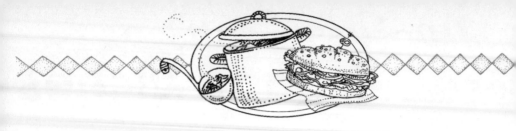

Yummy Soup Burgers

Judy Johnson
Bryant, AR

When my dad was in the Air Force, our family was stationed in France for three years. When we got back to the States, we stopped in Dallas to visit my aunt for a few days. She served us these burgers and we all loved them. Not only are they delicious, but they're so easy to make. It's not hard to see why they've been a favorite of our family for over two decades.

1 lb. ground beef
salt and pepper to taste
10-3/4 oz. can alphabet
   vegetable soup

8 hamburger buns, split
8 slices American cheese

In a skillet over medium heat, brown beef. Drain; add salt and pepper to taste. Stir in soup; cook until warmed through. Place bottom halves of buns on an ungreased baking sheet. Spoon beef mixture over buns; top each with a slice of cheese and add bun tops. Bake at 350 degrees for 5 to 10 minutes, until cheese is melted and buns are toasted. Makes 8 sandwiches.

Line the inside of a cabinet door with self-stick cork tiles to make a handy bulletin board. It'll be a great place to tack quick recipes, take-out menus, emergency numbers and more!

No-Fuss Soups
& Sandwiches

Spectacular Chicken Soup

Kathleen Sturm
Corona, CA

I concocted this recipe while babysitting for my five-year-old nephew, Dustin, who is rather a picky eater. Dustin loved this soup! I declared this recipe a keeper when he said between slurps, "Spectacular soup, Aunt Kat!" His parents were amazed later that night when I told them he had eaten three bowls for dinner.

1-1/2 c. celery, diced
1-1/2 c. carrot, peeled and diced
1/4 c. oil
2 T. onion powder

2 T. celery leaves, finely chopped
2 c. cooked chicken, diced
2 49-oz. cans chicken broth
1 c. orzo pasta, cooked

In a large soup pot over medium heat, sauté celery and carrot in oil. Drain; sprinkle with onion powder. Add celery leaves, chicken and broth; heat through. Spoon cooked pasta into individual soup bowls; ladle hot soup over top. Serves 6 to 8.

Use mini cookie cutters to make whimsical soup croutons... kids will love them! Cut out fun shapes from slices of day-old bread, brush with butter and bake at 200 degrees until croutons are crunchy and golden.

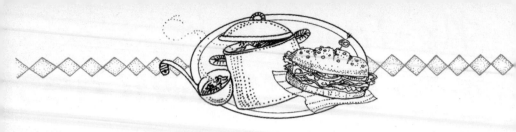

Hot Ham Rollers

Martha Stephens
Sibley, LA

For something different that kids will eat, these rolled-up sandwiches are easy to make and sure to please. Just add a side of fresh fruit and some chips for a yummy light meal.

20-oz. loaf honey wheat bread   1/3 c. olive oil, divided
1 lb. deli smoked ham
8-oz. pkg. shredded Cheddar
   cheese

On each slice of bread, place one slice of ham; sprinkle with cheese. Roll up. Place rolled sandwiches seam-side down on a baking sheet lightly brushed with olive oil. Brush each sandwich lightly with remaining oil. Bake at 350 degrees for 10 minutes; broil for 2 minutes to lightly toast sandwiches. Serves 6.

Making deviled eggs for supper? Whip 'em up in no time by combining ingredients in a plastic zipping bag instead of a bowl. Blend by squeezing the bag, snip off a corner and pipe the filling into the whites...no muss, no fuss!

No-Fuss Soups & Sandwiches

Farmers' Market Soup

Jason Keller
Carrollton, GA

We just love this veggie-packed soup! Sometimes I'll use quick-cooking barley instead of noodles, adding it at the same time as the fresh veggies.

2 c. cabbage, chopped
1 c. tomatoes, chopped
1/2 c. onion, chopped
1 c. zucchini or yellow squash, chopped
2 c. tomato juice
1 c. water

2 cubes beef bouillon
1 t. chili powder
1/2 t. celery seed
salt and pepper to taste
1 c. Kielbasa sausage, sliced and browned
1 c. thin egg noodles, cooked

In a stockpot over medium heat, combine all ingredients except sausage and noodles. Bring to a boil; reduce heat. Simmer, covered, for 45 minutes to one hour, until vegetables are tender. Add more juice or water, as needed. Stir in sausage and cooked noodles; heat through before serving. Makes 6 servings.

Get together with friends, neighbors and family for a soup supper. Each family brings a favorite soup to share, along with the recipe. What a delicious way to try a variety of soups and maybe find a new favorite!

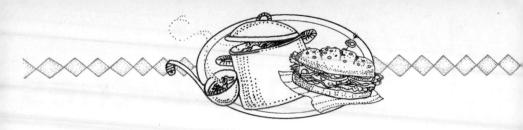

Spicy Sloppy Joes

Cindy Masterson
Grass Valley, CA

*I've been making these Sloppy Joes since 1966. My mom
and I used to double the recipe for my brother and his college
friends...it's still a favorite!*

1 lb. ground beef	12-oz. bottle chili sauce
1 onion, finely chopped	4 to 6 hamburger buns
2 stalks celery, finely chopped	

In a skillet over medium heat, brown beef; drain. Add onion and
celery and sauté. Stir in chili sauce and simmer for about 15 minutes.
Serve on hamburger buns. Makes 4 to 6 sandwiches.

Mini choppers make prep work a breeze for
chopping onions, celery, green peppers and
tomatoes...what a timesaver!

Fresh Mushroom Soup

Shirley Faist
Fremont, OH

I found this recipe in a magazine and I tried it because we love mushrooms and onions. It's easy to make, and I've passed the recipe to lots of people. It's very, very good!

3 T. margarine
8-oz. pkg. sliced mushrooms
2 onions, chopped
Optional: 2 stalks celery,
  chopped
3 T. all-purpose flour
6 c. chicken broth

1/3 c. long-cooking rice,
  uncooked
salt and pepper to taste
garlic powder to taste
Optional: 1 bay leaf
Garnish: 2 T. dried parsley

Melt margarine in a large saucepan over low heat. Add mushrooms, onion and celery, if using. Cook and stir over low heat for 5 minutes. Blend in flour. Add broth; increase heat to medium and cook, stirring constantly, until boiling. Reduce heat; add rice, seasonings and bay leaf, if desired. Cover and simmer for 20 minutes, or until rice is tender. Discard bay leaf, if using; sprinkle with parsley before serving. Makes 6 servings.

Need to add a little zing to a soup or stew? Just add a splash of Worcestershire sauce, lemon juice or cider vinegar.

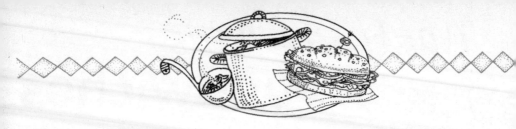

Ham & Cheese Calzones

Cindy Clauson
Rochester, IN

A terrific way to use up leftover baked ham! The directions may look complicated, but this recipe goes together quickly.

2 10-inch tubes refrigerated pizza crust
1 c. ricotta cheese, divided
6-oz. pkg. sliced pepperoni, divided
2 c. cooked ham, diced and divided

2 c. shredded mozzarella cheese, divided
Optional: grated Parmesan cheese, dried basil
Garnish: warm marinara sauce

Unroll one pizza crust and stretch gently to make a 14-inch by 11-inch rectangle. Spread half the ricotta over half the dough, lengthwise to within one inch of the edges. Over the ricotta-topped dough, sprinkle half the pepperoni, half the ham and half the mozzarella. Fold the unfilled half of dough over the filled half; press edges together firmly to seal. Transfer to a greased baking sheet. Repeat with remaining crust and filling ingredients. Bake at 400 degrees for 20 minutes, or until golden. Sprinkle with Parmesan and basil, if desired. Slice into serving-size pieces. Serve with marinara sauce. Makes 8 servings.

Declare a Picnic Night at home! Just toss a checkered tablecloth on the dinner table and set out paper plates and disposable plastic utensils. Relax and enjoy dinner...no dishes to wash!

No-Fuss Soups & Sandwiches

Oh-So-Easy Corn Chowder

Susan Owens
Redlands, CA

This satisfying soup goes together in a snap! Garnish individual servings with sour cream and chopped chives, if you like.

2 15-oz. cans new potatoes, drained and diced
2 15-oz. cans creamed corn
15-oz. can corn, drained
16-oz. can chicken, drained
2-oz. jar chopped pimentos, drained
salt and pepper to taste

Mix all ingredients in a stockpot over medium heat. Cook until bubbly and heated through. Serves 6.

Crunchy tortilla strips are a tasty addition to southwestern-style soups. Cut corn tortillas into thin strips, then deep-fry quickly. Drain on paper towels before sprinkling over bowls of soup.

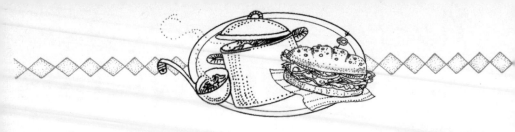

Vegetarian Corn Chili

Jennifer Parrish
Betterton, MD

*My husband and I love this chili served with a side of Spanish rice.
My daughter loves it with cornbread. It is a very simple recipe
for a lazy day.*

14-1/2 oz. can diced tomatoes
  with Italian herbs
16-oz. pkg. frozen sweet corn

15-oz. can vegetarian chili with
  beans

Combine all ingredients in a saucepan over medium heat. Cook,
stirring occasionally, until heated through and corn is cooked, about
10 minutes. Serves 4.

Crisp, savory oyster crackers are delightful
topping a steamy bowl of chili...see pages 44 and 64
for some quick-to-fix recipes.

Speedy Sides
& Salads

Stoplight Salad

Lori Boulay
Brunswick, ME

This colorful salad is oh-so easy to make and delicious to eat.
Perfect for potlucks!

3 eggs, hard-boiled, peeled
   and diced
10-oz. pkg. frozen peas, thawed
16-oz. pkg. frozen corn, thawed
2-oz. jar diced pimentos,
   drained

1 onion, diced
1/2 c. mayonnaise
seasoned salt to taste

In a large serving bowl, toss together all ingredients. Serve immediately or refrigerate. Makes 8 to 10 servings.

If time's short, pick up a bag of mixed salad greens
from the grocery and toss on a variety of favorite toppings
to make it special. Try crumbled blue or feta cheese,
sweetened dried cranberries, diced apples and
chopped walnuts...yum!

Speedy Sides
& Salads

Easy Layered Salad

Debbie Worthington
Bainbridge, GA

Packed full of tasty ingredients, this salad is always a hit.

12-oz. pkg. salad mix with
   iceberg lettuce and carrots
15-oz. can peas, drained
8-oz. can sliced water chestnuts,
   drained
1 red pepper, diced
8-oz. pkg. shredded Cheddar
   cheese

1-1/2 c. mayonnaise
1 t. sugar
3-oz. pkg. bacon bits
1/2 c. shredded Parmesan
   cheese

In a large serving bowl, layer ingredients in the following order: salad mix, peas, water chestnuts, red pepper and Cheddar cheese. Mix together mayonnaise and sugar; spread over layers. Sprinkle bacon bits and Parmesan cheese over top. Cover and chill before serving. Makes 10 to 12 servings.

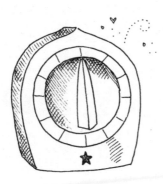

For hearty salads in a snap, keep unopened cans and jars of diced tomatoes, olives, garbanzo beans and marinated artichokes in the fridge. They'll be chilled and ready to toss with fresh greens or cooked pasta at a moment's notice.

Better Than Creamed Corn

Cindy DeMay
West Springfield, MA

*This is the dish I'm always asked to bring to any family gathering!
With just four ingredients, I'm happy to.*

12-oz. pkg. frozen corn
1/2 c. brown sugar, packed

1 c. sour cream
1/4 c. grated Parmesan cheese

In an ungreased 8"x8" baking pan, layer all ingredients in order given.
Cover and bake at 350 degrees for 20 minutes. Stir to mix before
serving. Makes 4 to 6 servings.

A quick and tasty side dish! Roll balls of
leftover mashed potatoes in a mixture of grated
Parmesan cheese and seasoned dry bread
crumbs...broil until golden.

Yummy Yellow Squash

Marci Muir
Port Huron, MI

This is my kids' favorite side dish...any recipe that gets them to eat their veggies is a winner in my book!

1 T. butter
3 lbs. yellow squash, thinly
  sliced

1 onion, sliced
1 to 2 T. garlic salt

Place butter and squash in a large skillet over medium heat. Cover and cook until butter has melted, about 3 minutes, stirring occasionally. Add onion to skillet and stir. Cook for 5 to 7 minutes, stirring occasionally. Sprinkle with garlic salt to taste. Cook an additional 5 to 7 minutes, until squash is tender. Serves 4 to 6.

Steam veggies to keep their fresh-picked taste...it's easy!
Bring 1/2 inch of water to a boil in a saucepan and
add cut-up veggies. Cover and cook for 3 to 5 minutes,
to desired tenderness. A quick toss with a little
butter and they're ready to serve.

Parmesan-Stuffed Tomatoes
Kimberly Horstman
Byron Center, MI

I make this every fall with sun-ripe tomatoes from my garden. It is so fast and tastes wonderful...try it, you'll love it too!

4 tomatoes, tops removed
1 c. quick-cooking rice,
  uncooked
1 c. grated Parmesan cheese
1/4 c. margarine, melted
1/4 c. fresh basil, chopped

1 t. garlic, minced
1 t. salt
1/4 t. pepper
Garnish: Parmesan cheese,
  fresh parsley

Scoop out tomato pulp, leaving a 1/4-inch shell; coarsely chop pulp. Place tomatoes in an ungreased microwave-safe dish. Mix tomato pulp with rice, cheese, margarine and seasonings. Spoon mixture into tomatoes; spoon any remaining mixture into center of dish. Cover with vented plastic wrap. Microwave on high for 5 minutes, until rice is tender. Garnish as desired. Serves 4.

E-Z Cheesy Cauliflower
Dianne Young
South Jordan, UT

My quick go-to side when company drops by for supper.

1 head cauliflower, chopped
1/2 c. water
1/4 c. mayonnaise-type salad
  dressing

1/4 t. onion salt
1/2 t. mustard
1/2 to 1 c. shredded Cheddar
  cheese

Place cauliflower and water in an ungreased microwave-safe dish. Cover loosely with plastic wrap and microwave on high for 5 to 6 minutes, or until tender; drain. Combine dressing, salt and mustard; stir into cauliflower. Top with cheese; microwave an additional 30 seconds, until cheese is melted. Serves 4 to 6.

Speedy Sides & Salads

Veggie "Fried" Rice

Barb Rudyk
Alberta, Canada

A tasty, easy-to-make side that's similar to fried rice...without the frying! For added flavor, toss in a beef or chicken bouillon cube instead of the salt.

1-1/2 c. long-cooking rice,
   uncooked
1/2 c. carrots, peeled and finely
   diced
1/2 c. celery, finely diced
1/2 c. onion, finely diced
3 c. water
1 t. salt

Place all ingredients in a heavy saucepan over medium heat. Bring to a boil. Cover and boil gently about 15 minutes, until rice is tender and water is absorbed. Serves 4.

A flexible plastic cutting mat makes speedy work of slicing & dicing. Keep two mats on hand for chopping veggies and meat separately.

Mary's Macaroni & Cheese

Mary Casasanta
Tracy, CA

This is awesome mac & cheese...good enough to be the main dish!

16-oz. pkg. elbow macaroni,
   cooked
1/2 c. butter, diced
16-oz. container sharp Cheddar
   cheese spread
2 c. shredded Colby Jack cheese

2 eggs, beaten
12-oz. can evaporated milk
1 c. shredded Cheddar cheese
1 c. panko bread crumbs or
   plain dry bread crumbs

In a large bowl, mix together all ingredients except Cheddar cheese
and bread crumbs. Pour into a greased 13"x9" baking pan. Top with
Cheddar cheese and bread crumbs. Bake, uncovered, at 350 degrees
for 30 minutes, until bubbly and golden. Makes 10 servings.

FRESH FRUIT
Since 1938

A big chalkboard in the kitchen is a handy spot
to keep a running grocery list.

Speedy Spanish Rice

Jocelyn Medina
Phoenixville, PA

An old favorite that we still enjoy. If you don't have a small-size can
of tomato juice on hand, just measure 3/4 cup tomato juice.

1 c. long-cooking rice, uncooked	1/2 t. garlic powder
1/2 c. onion, chopped	1/2 t. chili powder
2 T. oil	1/2 t. ground cumin
2 c. chicken broth	1/3 c. fresh cilantro, chopped
5-1/2 oz. can tomato juice	

In a skillet over medium heat, sauté rice and onion in oil until onion
is crisp-tender. Add remaining ingredients except cilantro. Bring to a
boil; reduce heat and cover. Simmer for 15 minutes, until liquid is
absorbed. Fluff rice with a fork; fold in cilantro. Serves 6.

Spoon leftover Spanish Rice into flour tortillas
for a yummy quick lunch. For the softest tortillas,
wrap them in a damp paper towel and
microwave for about 15 seconds.

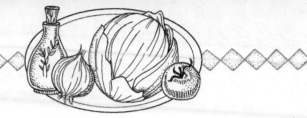

Gerry's Green Bean Bake

Teresa Amert
Upper Sandusky, OH

This recipe came from my sister, Gerry, who is an excellent cook. The sour cream and lemon juice make this casserole delicious.

4 c. green beans, trimmed and sliced
1 onion, finely chopped
1/4 c. plus 3 T. butter, melted and divided

1 c. sour cream
2 T. lemon juice
salt and pepper to taste
1/2 c. saltine crackers, crushed

In a large saucepan, cover green beans with water. Cook over medium heat just until tender, about 15 minutes; drain. Meanwhile, in a separate small saucepan over medium heat, sauté onion in 1/4 cup butter until tender. In a bowl, mix together green beans, sour cream, lemon juice and onion mixture. Transfer to a buttered 2-quart casserole dish. Mix together crackers and remaining butter in a small bowl. Sprinkle over green bean mixture. Bake, uncovered, at 375 degrees for 20 minutes. Serves 6.

Brighten a dinner plate with edible fruit and veggie garnishes...try carrot curls, radish roses, pineapple spears or kiwi slices.

Creamy Spinach Supreme

Elsie Kleiber
Marysville, OH

The cheesiest, most scrumptious spinach casserole ever.

2 10-oz. pkgs. frozen chopped
   spinach, thawed and drained
2 c. shredded Monterey Jack
   cheese

10-3/4 oz. can cream of potato
   soup
1 c. sour cream
1/2 c. grated Parmesan cheese

In a large bowl, combine all ingredients; mix well. Transfer to a greased 11"x7" baking pan. Bake, uncovered, at 325 degrees for 25 to 30 minutes, until bubbly and edges are lightly golden. Makes 4 to 6 servings.

When you're putting away the groceries, label ingredients before refrigerating so they won't become snacks instead. Cheese cubes, fruit and veggies labeled "OK for snacking" are sure to tame appetites without upsetting your dinner plans.

Sweet Carrot Delight

Libby Case
Shepherdsville, KY

Years ago, my uncle shared this recipe with me and it's become a family favorite. You can't beat it with burgers or barbecued chicken at cookouts...it even goes well with turkey & dressing.

16-oz. pkg. baby carrots
21-oz. can apple pie filling

1 t. cinnamon
2 T. butter, sliced

In a saucepan over medium-high heat, cover carrots with water. Bring to a boil and cook until tender, about 7 to 8 minutes; drain. Mix carrots and pie filling in a 2-quart casserole dish sprayed with non-stick vegetable spray. Sprinkle with cinnamon; mix gently. Dot with pats of butter. Cover and bake at 325 degrees for 20 to 25 minutes, until bubbly. Makes 6 to 8 servings.

Save time when peeling and chopping veggies.
Set a large bowl on the counter to toss all the peelings
into...you'll only need to empty it once.

Cordie's Spicy Baked Beans

Pat Beach
Fisherville, KY

My mother created this recipe over forty years ago...ever since, we have served these scrumptious baked beans at our family get-togethers. Now my daughters enjoy preparing this recipe with their children.

1/2 lb. ground pork sausage	1/2 c. catsup
1/2 green pepper, chopped	1/3 c. brown sugar, packed
1/2 onion, chopped	1 T. chili powder
2 15-oz. cans pork & beans, drained	1 t. mustard

In a large saucepan over medium heat, brown sausage with green pepper and onion; drain. Add remaining ingredients; mix well. Simmer for 15 minutes over medium heat, stirring frequently. Makes 4 to 6 servings.

The best things in life aren't things.
-Art Buchwald

Instant Pierogies

Jackie Balla
Walbridge, OH

Buttery noodles and sauerkraut...ready in a jiffy and wonderful served alongside pork chops or smoked sausage.

16-oz. pkg. frozen egg noodles
1 sweet onion, sliced

1/2 c. butter
27-oz. can sauerkraut, drained

Prepare frozen noodles according to package directions. Drain; keep warm. In a skillet over medium heat, sauté onion in butter. In a separate saucepan, simmer sauerkraut over medium heat. Combine all ingredients; toss well and serve hot. Makes 8 to 10 servings.

Fresh veggies don't need to be fussy. Set out a platter of bite-size veggies along with a super-simple creamy dip made by blending one cup cottage cheese, 1/4 cup plain yogurt, one tablespoon minced onion, one teaspoon dried parsley and 1/4 teaspoon dill weed. Yum!

Speedy Sides & Salads

Baby Peas & Mushrooms

Sherry Henry
Moran, KS

When I was a girl, our 4-H foods leader asked us to bring a microwave recipe to our next meeting. This is the delicious recipe that my friend brought. Since then, I've been taking it to dinners and potlucks for over 25 years. The dish always comes home empty!

2 10-oz. pkgs. frozen peas
2 4-oz. cans sliced mushrooms,
　　drained
1/2 onion, diced

2 T. butter, sliced
2 T. soy sauce
2 T. sugar
salt and pepper to taste

In a 2-quart microwave-safe dish, mix all ingredients together. Cover loosely with plastic wrap and microwave on high for 11 minutes, stirring halfway through. Serves 8.

For recipes with fresh-picked flavor year 'round, keep a pot of chives, parsley or thyme growing on the windowsill...ready to snip as needed.

Artichokes & Spirals Salad

Carol Lytle
Columbus, OH

There's nothing better in the summer than a cool pasta salad, unless it's pasta salad with artichokes! I tossed this together one day for a potluck with items I had on hand. What a hit! I have made it dozens of times since...it's so easy and so delicious!

16-oz. pkg. rotini pasta,
  uncooked
1 bunch broccoli, cut into
  flowerets
1 red pepper, thinly sliced

6-1/2 oz. jar marinated
  artichokes, drained and
  marinade reserved
1/4 c. grated Parmesan cheese
salt and pepper to taste

Cook rotini according to package directions, adding broccoli in final 2 minutes. Drain; rinse with cold water. In a large serving bowl, combine all ingredients, adding reserved marinade to taste. Toss to mix; cover and chill before serving. Serves 8.

Sweet-and-Sour Tomatoes

Darrell Lawry
Kissimmee, FL

A perfect dish to make when you've got a surplus of homegrown tomatoes in your garden. I like to add chopped fresh basil if I have some in the garden as well.

7 tomatoes, thinly sliced
1 onion, thinly sliced
1/2 c. sugar

1/2 c. white vinegar
1/2 c. oil
salt and pepper to taste

In a large bowl, toss together all ingredients until well mixed. Serve at room temperature. Refrigerate any leftovers. Makes 8 servings.

Broccoli-Bacon Toss

Rose Griep
Oil City, PA

A local restaurant that closed its doors ten years ago used to feature this salad on their buffet. This is my version...I think I finally got it right! Be sure to finely chop the broccoli and onion so that each forkful has a little taste of each of the ingredients.

1 bunch broccoli, finely chopped
1 onion, finely diced
3-1/2 oz. pkg. bacon bits

3/4 c. shredded Cheddar cheese
1/2 c. sunflower kernels
1 c. currants

In a large serving bowl, mix together all ingredients. Drizzle with Parmesan Dressing; toss to coat lightly. Serves 10 to 12.

Parmesan Dressing:

2 c. mayonnaise
1/2 c. sugar

1/4 c. grated Parmesan cheese

Mix together all ingredients in a small bowl.

Some recipes only call for half an onion, so save time on a future recipe...just chop the other half and freeze it right away.

Delicious Dilled Carrots

Irene Robinson
Cincinnati, OH

My family just loves these carrots...they go well with any entrée.

1 lb. carrots, peeled and thinly
   sliced
1/2 c. celery, thinly sliced
1/4 c. onion, chopped
1/4 c. white wine or chicken
   broth

2 T. sugar
2 T. margarine
1/8 t. dill weed

Combine all ingredients in a large saucepan. Cover and cook over medium heat for 10 to 15 minutes, stirring occasionally, until vegetables are fork-tender. Serves 4.

A baked sweet potato is an easy side just about everyone will love. Bake at 375 degrees until tender, about 40 to 45 minutes, then top with a little butter and cinnamon-sugar.

Fully-Loaded Mashed Potatoes   *Norma Burton*
Kuna, ID

*I was going to prepare individual baked potatoes for dinner
but needed to hurry, so I mashed all the ingredients together
instead...everyone loved it!*

6 potatoes, peeled and quartered
1/4 c. butter, softened
1/2 c. sour cream
1/2 t. salt
1/8 t. pepper

4 slices bacon, crisply cooked
    and crumbled
1/2 c. shredded Cheddar cheese
4 green onions, thinly sliced

Put potatoes in a saucepan and cover with water. Bring to a boil
over medium-high heat; reduce heat and cover. Simmer for 15 to
20 minutes, until fork-tender; drain. Mash potatoes with a potato
masher or an electric mixer on low speed. Add butter, sour cream, salt
and pepper; mash until fluffy. Mix in remaining ingredients. Makes
6 servings.

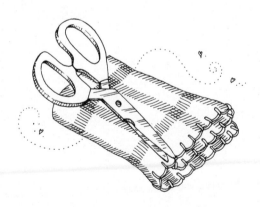

Keep a pair of kitchen scissors handy for chopping bacon,
snipping green onions and opening packages...you'll
wonder what you ever did without them!

Rainbow Pasta Salad

Robin Weaver
Bronston, KY

This recipe was given to me by a family member more than twenty years ago, before I was married...I've been making it ever since. I like to make this salad in the summer when garden-fresh vegetables are abundant...it really makes a difference in the flavor!

16-oz. pkg. tri-color rotini
   pasta, uncooked
1 cucumber, thinly sliced
1 green pepper, thinly sliced

1 onion, thinly sliced
3 tomatoes, chopped
Optional: diced Cheddar cheese,
   sliced pepperoni

Cook rotini according to package directions; drain and rinse with cold water. Combine with remaining ingredients in a large serving bowl; toss to mix. Drizzle with Cider Vinegar Dressing to taste. Cover and chill; toss again before serving. Makes 12 servings.

Cider Vinegar Dressing:

3/4 c. oil
1-1/2 c. sugar
1-1/2 c. cider vinegar
2 T. mustard
1 T. garlic salt

1 T. dried parsley
1 t. salt
1-1/2 t. pepper
Optional: 1 T. flavor enhancer

Whisk together all ingredients in a medium bowl.

Combine the ingredients for this simple salad dressing
in a squeeze bottle instead of a bowl. Shake the
bottle to incorporate flavors and squeeze onto
salad...what could be easier?

Flavorful Corn Salad

Cindy Martin
Wanette, OK

This yummy salad is requested at every family get-together and our community fish fries. I have given out this recipe hundreds of times... people are always amazed to learn how simple it is to make!

4 11-oz. cans sweet corn &
   diced peppers, drained
6 green onions, chopped
2 c. shredded mild Cheddar
   cheese

2 c. mayonnaise
23-oz. pkg. chili-flavored corn
   chips, crushed

In a large bowl, mix together all ingredients except chips. Cover and chill. At serving time, sprinkle corn chips on top. Serves 10 to 12.

Fresh Spinach Salad

Polly McCallum
Palatka, FL

Spinach, bacon and eggs...a classic salad combination.

3 eggs, hard-boiled, peeled and
   chopped
1/4 lb. bacon, crisply cooked
   and crumbled
9-oz. pkg. spinach, torn
1 c. herb-flavored stuffing mix
1/3 c. sugar

1/3 c. vinegar
1/3 c. oil
1 T. mustard
1 t. celery seed
1 t. salt
1/2 t. pepper
1 onion, chopped

Mix together eggs, bacon, spinach and stuffing mix in a large bowl. For dressing, whisk together remaining ingredients except onion. Stir in onion just before serving. Toss with dressing at serving time. Serves 6.

Rosemary Roasted Potatoes

Penny Sherman
Cumming, GA

This is the easiest potato dish ever, yet it's packed with flavor!
You don't even need to peel the potatoes.

2 lbs. redskin potatoes, diced
1/4 c. olive oil
1 t. dried rosemary
1 t. onion powder

1/2 t. garlic salt
1/2 t. pepper
1/4 t. paprika

Place potatoes in a greased 13"x9" baking pan; set aside. Mix
remaining ingredients in a small bowl; drizzle over potatoes and toss
to coat. Bake, uncovered, at 325 degrees for 30 minutes. Stir; bake
an additional 10 minutes, until potatoes are tender and golden. Makes
6 to 8 servings.

For a delicious, healthy side that practically cooks itself, fill
aluminum foil packets with sliced fresh veggies. Top with
seasoning salt and two ice cubes, seal and bake at
450 degrees for 20 to 25 minutes, until tender.

Speedy Sides
& Salads

Country-Style Pepper Cabbage

Tonya Adams
Magnolia, KY

*My mother used to fix this simple side for
my grandfather...it's still a favorite!*

4 c. cabbage, thinly sliced
1/4 c. onion, chopped
1 c. milk
3 T. butter

1 t. sugar
1/2 t. salt
1/4 t. pepper

Combine all ingredients in a 2-quart stockpot over medium heat.
Cover and boil for 5 to 10 minutes; do not overcook. Serve piping hot.
Serves 4.

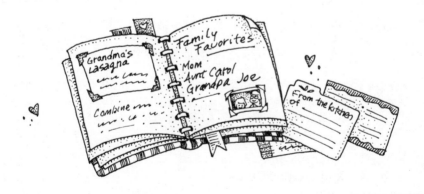

Take time to share family stories and traditions with your
kids over the dinner table! A cherished family recipe
can be a super conversation starter.

Mountain Momma's Corn

Jill Palmer
Tollgate, OR

A simple recipe, but oh-so good!

12-oz. pkg. frozen corn
1 T. butter, sliced

3-oz. pkg. cream cheese,
softened and cubed

In a saucepan, cook corn according to package directions; drain. Add butter and cream cheese; stir until melted. Serves 4 to 6.

Savory Yellow Snap Beans

Debbie Jurczyk
Gilbertville, MA

When I was first married thirty years ago, my mother-in-law taught me to prepare snap beans this way. My husband can make a meal of a huge plate of these delicious beans!

3 lbs. yellow snap beans,
   trimmed and snapped into
   bite-size pieces
1/4 c. butter, softened
3/4 c. round buttery crackers,
   crushed

1 t. seasoned salt
1/2 t. garlic powder
1/8 t. pepper

In a large saucepan over medium heat, cover beans with water. Bring to a boil; cook until tender, about 20 minutes. Drain; add butter and stir to coat. Toss together with remaining ingredients and serve immediately. Serves 6.

Must-Have Asparagus Bake

Glenda Ballard
West Columbia, SC

*My family likes this casserole so much, we've actually drawn straws
to see who would get the last serving!*

15-oz. can asparagus spears,
   drained and divided
2 c. shredded Cheddar cheese,
   divided
10-3/4 oz. can cream of
   mushroom soup, divided

3/4 c. dry bread crumbs
1 T. butter, sliced

In a one-quart casserole dish coated with non-stick vegetable spray,
layer half the asparagus, half the cheese and half the soup. Repeat
layers. Top with bread crumbs; dot with butter. Bake, uncovered, at
350 degrees for 20 minutes, until golden on top and cheese is melted.
Serves 4.

What could be faster than "shopping" for veggies just
outside the kitchen door? Even the smallest yard is sure to
have a sunny corner where you can grow sun-ripened
tomatoes, lots of zucchini and an herb plant or two.

Stovetop Broccoli Casserole

Kelly Gray
Weston, WV

My mama used to make this dish and I just loved it. It is so simple to make, but I thought she was a gourmet chef! It only takes one pan and fifteen minutes to fix.

2 16-oz. pkgs. frozen broccoli
   flowerets
2 c. shredded mild Cheddar
   cheese

5-oz. pkg. croutons
2 to 3 t. garlic salt
1 t. pepper
2 T. butter

In a saucepan, cook broccoli according to package directions; drain and return to pan. Add cheese; cook and stir over medium-low heat until it starts to melt. Stir in croutons, garlic salt and pepper. Add butter and cook an additional 5 to 10 minutes, until heated through. Serves 8.

For a scrumptious quick side or light main, bake up a quiche. Place a cup of chopped cooked veggies in a pie crust, then whisk together 3 eggs and a small can of evaporated milk. Add one cup shredded cheese. Pour into crust and bake at 400 degrees until set, 20 to 25 minutes. A great way to use leftovers!

Easy Bacon Frittata, page 21

Country Sausage Gravy, page 18

Morning Glory Muffins, page 16

Pigs in the Clover, page 22

Julie's Fresh Guacamole, page 41

Honey-BBQ Chicken Wings, page 48

Fresh Spinach Salad, page 121

E-Z Cheesy Cauliflower, page 106

Reuben Dip, page 64

Fully-Loaded Mashed Potatoes, page 119

Rainbow Pasta Salad, page 120

Hamburger Stroganoff, page 169

Garden Skillet Dinner with Chicken, page 168

Creamy Chicken & Biscuits, page 141

Barb's Bacon Green Beans, page 128

Rosemary Roasted Potatoes, page 122

Aunt Mary's Calico Beans, page 129

Broccoli Salad Deluxe, page 130

Quick Peanut Butter Fudge, page 191

Sunny Lemon Blossoms, page 202

Cherry Crumb Dessert, page 197

Speedy Sides
& Salads

Cheesy Micro-Baked Potatoes

Kelly Marcum
Rock Falls, IL

The first year my husband planted a garden, we had a bumper crop of potatoes. So I invented the easiest way to update our family's favorite, the baked potato. These are simply delicious!

4 to 6 baking potatoes
1/2 c. margarine, sliced
2 c. shredded Cheddar cheese

Garnish: sour cream, bacon bits, chopped fresh chives

Pierce potatoes with a fork; place in microwave. Cover with plastic and microwave on high for 10 to 12 minutes, until fork-tender. Carefully cut hot potatoes into quarters. Arrange potatoes in a large microwave-safe dish that has been sprayed with non-stick vegetable spray. Dot with margarine and cover with cheese. Microwave on high, uncovered, an additional 10 minutes, until hot and bubbly. Garnish as desired. Serves 4 to 6.

Whip up a homemade salt-free seasoning that's tasty on all kinds of veggies and meats. Combine one tablespoon each dried oregano, basil and pepper, 1-1/2 teaspoons each onion powder and thyme and one teaspoon garlic powder. Fill a large shaker container to keep by the stove.

Barb's Bacon Green Beans

LaShelle Brown
Mulvane, KS

My Aunt Barb is a wonderful cook...I'm happy to share this simple recipe of hers! It's an easy way to dress up plain old canned beans.

3 slices bacon, quartered
1-1/2 T. onion, chopped
1 clove garlic, chopped
14-1/2 oz. can green beans,
   drained

1 T. soy sauce
Optional: diced tomato, 1/2 c.
   shredded Cheddar cheese

In a skillet over medium heat, cook bacon until crisp. Drain most of the drippings, reserving one tablespoon in skillet. Add onion and garlic; sauté for 2 minutes. Add green beans and soy sauce to bacon mixture. Toss until coated and heated through. Top with diced tomato and cheese, if desired. Makes 4 servings.

Warm garlic bread makes any meal a little better!
Blend together 1/2 cup softened butter with 2 minced garlic cloves, one tablespoon chopped parsley and 1/4 cup grated Parmesan cheese. Spread over Italian bread halves, broil 2 to 3 minutes until golden and bubbly. Slice and serve...mmm!

Aunt Mary's Calico Beans

Marlys Patterson
Denver, IA

A favorite elderly aunt of my husband's used to bring this dish to the annual family reunion. It was always so tasty that we named it for her. It is easy to make, inexpensive and makes a generous portion for a family meal or for a carry-in dinner.

1/2 lb. ground beef
1 c. onion, diced
1/2 lb. bacon, cut into bite-size pieces
15-oz. can pork & beans
15-oz. can kidney beans, partially drained

15-oz. can butter beans, partially drained
3/4 c. brown sugar, packed
1/2 c. catsup
2 t. vinegar
1 t. dry mustard
1/2 t. salt

Brown beef and onion in a deep, heavy iron skillet over medium heat; drain. Add bacon to beef mixture; continue cooking until bacon is done but not crisp. Do not drain. Add remaining ingredients and stir well. Simmer, uncovered, over very low heat for 20 to 30 minutes, stirring frequently. Makes 10 to 12 servings.

Keep a couple of favorite side dishes tucked away in the freezer for busy days. Pair with hot sandwiches or a deli roast chicken to put a hearty homestyle meal on the table in a hurry.

Broccoli Salad Deluxe

*Maggie Peck
Plano, TX*

Our family especially loves this salad during the holiday season! The cranberries, apricots and almonds make it extra yummy. This is a great party pleaser...very convenient since it can be made ahead.

1 c. mayonnaise
1/4 c. sugar
1/4 c. red wine vinegar
1/4 t. salt
1/4 t. pepper
1-1/2 lbs. broccoli, cut into
   flowerets and chopped
1/2 red onion, diced

6-oz. pkg. sweetened dried
   cranberries
2-1/4 oz. pkg. slivered almonds,
   toasted
3/8 c. dried apricots, diced
1/2 c. shredded extra-sharp
   Cheddar cheese

Whisk together mayonnaise, sugar, vinegar, salt and pepper in a large bowl. Add remaining ingredients; toss together. Serve immediately or cover and chill up to 6 hours before serving. Makes 8 to 10 servings.

Avoid soggy salads...simply pour salad dressing in the bottom of a salad bowl, then add greens on top. Toss just before serving...fresh and crisp!

Sunshine Coleslaw

Shelley LaDue
Victoria, Australia

This colorful salad came about one day when I needed to use the ingredients that I had on hand. The result was really flavorful!

5 c. cabbage, shredded
2 carrots, peeled and sliced
1/2 c. corn
1/4 c. Thousand Island salad
  dressing

3 T. ranch salad dressing
3 T. lemon-herb salad dressing
salt and pepper to taste
Garnish: fresh parsley, chopped

In a salad bowl, toss together cabbage, carrots, corn and salad dressings. Add salt and pepper to taste. Garnish with parsley before serving. Makes 8 servings.

Serve up individual portions of coleslaw or pasta salad in edible bowls! Hollow out fresh green, yellow or red peppers and fill 'em up with salad for a quick and tasty lunch.

Special Vegetable Bake

Linda Griffin
Roanoke, VA

I first tasted this casserole when friends brought food to our home after my mother had passed away. It was so yummy that we just had to get the recipe. Couldn't be easier or more delicious!

3 15-oz. cans mixed vegetables, drained
8-oz. jar pasteurized process cheese sauce
1/2 c. butter, melted
1/3 c. round buttery cracker crumbs

Mix together all ingredients except cracker crumbs; transfer to a greased 2-quart casserole dish. Sprinkle with cracker crumbs. Bake, uncovered, at 350 degrees for 30 minutes. Makes 10 to 12 servings.

Get together with a girlfriend or two and spend a day making double batches of favorite casseroles to freeze. Your freezers will be full of homemade meals in no time!

Speedy Sides & Salads

Yummy Potato Goo

Kathleen Popp
Oak Harbor, WA

Spoon this topping onto baked potatoes...scrumptious!

1/2 c. butter, softened
3/4 c. sour cream

1 c. shredded Cheddar cheese

Blend butter, sour cream and cheese together. Use immediately or keep refrigerated. Makes 4 servings.

Micro-Quick Potato Sticks

Irene Whatling
West Des Moines, IA

When I started a diet, I soon found this recipe that the whole family could enjoy. It's a healthy change from French fries...good with anything from burgers on the grill to pot roast!

3 baking potatoes, each cut into
   8 wedges
3 T. grated Parmesan cheese

2 t. dried oregano
2 t. paprika
1 t. garlic powder

Spray potatoes lightly with non-stick vegetable spray and set aside. Combine remaining ingredients in a large plastic zipping bag. Add potatoes; shake to coat. Transfer potatoes to a microwave-safe dish coated with non-stick vegetable spray. Cover loosely; microwave on high for 6 minutes. Turn dish halfway; microwave an additional 4 to 6 minutes, until potatoes are tender. Serves 3 to 4.

Tangy Apple Salad

Suzanne Bayorgeon
Norfolk, NY

*A family favorite for picnics and barbecues. Add color to the salad
by leaving the apples unpeeled...save time too!*

5 McIntosh or Granny Smith
   apples, cored and cut into
   bite-size pieces

3/4 c. red onion, diced
1/2 c. crumbled blue cheese
1 c. zesty Italian salad dressing

Mix together all ingredients in a large serving bowl. Serve immediately
or refrigerate for 2 to 3 hours. Serves 6 to 8.

Homemade Applesauce

Lisa Neece
Olalla, WA

Our family loves this tart-sweet applesauce in chilly weather.

6 Granny Smith apples, cored,
   peeled and sliced

1/2 c. sugar
cinnamon to taste

Place apples in a medium saucepan with just enough water to cover
them; add sugar. Cook over medium-high heat for 10 to 15 minutes.
Let cool; mash to desired consistency. Add cinnamon to taste. Makes
4 servings.

A potato masher is useful for lots more than potatoes!
Mash apples for applesauce, mash bananas for
banana bread, even break up ground beef quickly
and evenly as it browns.

Speedy Sides & Salads

Spiced Oranges

Kim Hinshaw
Cedar Park, TX

An easy fruit side that can also be enjoyed as an unusual topping over a green salad or even ice cream. In a hurry? Substitute drained canned mandarin oranges.

1 T. powdered sugar
1 T. lemon juice
1/4 t. cinnamon
2-1/2 c. oranges, peeled and
    thinly sliced

1/4 c. slivered almonds
2-1/2 T. chopped dates

In a medium bowl, mix powdered sugar, lemon juice and cinnamon until well blended. Add oranges and toss to coat evenly. Cover and chill for 20 minutes. Just before serving, stir in almonds and dates. Makes 4 servings.

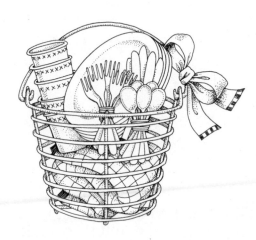

Pick up some paper plates and cups in seasonal designs...they'll make dinner fun when you're in a hurry and clean-up will be a breeze.

Fast Fruit Salad

Kathy White
Cato, NY

Add a rainbow of color to any meal! This salad has been a favorite of our family of ten for years because of its simplicity and low cost.

20-oz. can pineapple chunks
15-oz. can mandarin oranges,
   drained

1 red apple, cored and cubed
1 green apple, cored and cubed
1 c. seedless red grapes, halved

Combine undrained pineapple and remaining ingredients in a medium bowl. Stir well to coat apples with juice. Serve with a slotted spoon. Makes 6 to 8 servings.

If there's leftover salad after dinner, use it for a tasty sandwich filling the next day. Split a pita pocket, stuff with salad, chopped chicken or turkey, sliced grapes and drizzle with salad dressing.

Speedy Sides & Salads

Zesty Marinated Veggies

Amy Hunt
Traphill, NC

*A dear friend shared this speedy recipe with me when I needed
something quick for a last-minute church picnic.*

16-oz. pkg. frozen broccoli,
  carrots and cauliflower

1 red onion, sliced
1/2 c. Italian salad dressing

In a microwave-safe dish, microwave frozen vegetables on high until
tender, about half the cook time given on package directions. Drain
and add onion slices. Drizzle with salad dressing; refrigerate for 2
hours before serving. Serves 6.

Use a damp sponge sprinkled with baking soda to
scrub fruits & veggies...it works just as well as expensive
cleansers for vegetables.

Marinated Carrot Coins

Patricia Tiede
Cheektowaga, NY

My mom always made these carrots for special summer picnics in the backyard...it was one way she could get me to eat carrots! This goes together very quickly, but do make it the night before...the longer it marinates, the better it tastes.

2 lbs. carrots, peeled and sliced
10-3/4 oz. can tomato soup
1/2 c. white vinegar
1/2 c. oil
3/4 c. sugar

1 t. mustard
1 t. Worcestershire sauce
salt and pepper to taste
1 onion, thinly sliced
1 green pepper, chopped

Place carrots in a saucepan and cover with water. Cook over medium-high heat for 15 minutes, or until crisp-tender; drain. Meanwhile, in a separate saucepan, combine remaining ingredients. Bring to a boil over medium heat. Remove from heat and add carrots, mixing well. Refrigerate 24 hours before serving. Makes 8 to 10 servings.

Serve up a Southern-style vegetable plate for dinner. With two or three scrumptious veggie dishes and a basket of buttery cornbread, no one will miss the meat!

138

Dinner in a Dash

T's Saucy Skillet Meatloaves

Crystal Bruns
Iliff, CO

One of my two young boys' favorite meals! Just add some creamy mashed potatoes for a satisfying homestyle meal.

1-1/2 lbs. ground beef
1/2 c. dry bread crumbs
1 egg, beaten
10-3/4 oz. can tomato soup,
   divided
1/4 c. onion, chopped

1 t. salt
1 t. pepper
1/4 c. water
1/2 t. mustard
1/2 c. shredded mozzarella
   cheese

In a large bowl, combine beef, bread crumbs, egg, 1/4 cup soup, onion, salt and pepper. Mix well, using your hands; shape firmly into 2 loaves. Heat a large deep skillet over medium-high heat. Add meatloaves to skillet and brown on both sides; reduce heat to medium and cover with a lid. Simmer for about 25 minutes, or until beef is cooked through. Drain; stir in remaining soup, water and mustard. Top meatloaves with cheese. Simmer, uncovered, for 10 minutes, stirring sauce occasionally. Serves 6.

When mixing up a meatloaf, place all the ingredients in a large plastic zipping bag. Seal the bag and squish the bag until everything is well mixed...afterwards, just toss away the bag!

140

Dinner in a Dash

Creamy Chicken & Biscuits

Brenda Hager
Nancy, KY

My husband really enjoys this delicious dish. It's a wonderful comfort food meal but lightened up so we can enjoy it without the guilt!

2 c. new redskin potatoes,
　halved or quartered
2 c. carrots, peeled and sliced
1 onion, diced
3 T. butter
3 T. all-purpose flour
salt and pepper to taste
2 c. milk

1 c. low-sodium chicken broth
2 cubes low-sodium chicken
　bouillon
2 boneless, skinless chicken
　breasts, cooked and diced
12-oz. tube large refrigerated
　biscuits, cut into quarters

Cover potatoes, carrots and onion with water in a medium saucepan. Bring to a boil over medium heat; reduce heat and simmer until tender. Drain and set aside. Melt butter in another medium saucepan; stir in flour, salt and pepper, stirring constantly. Gradually add milk, broth and bouillon. Cook until thickened, about 3 to 5 minutes; set aside. Combine chicken and vegetables in a lightly greased 13"x9" baking pan. Pour sauce over top; arrange biscuits over sauce. Bake, uncovered, at 400 degrees for 15 minutes, or until biscuits are golden and sauce is bubbly. Serves 8.

Day-old bread is fine for making stuffing cubes and casserole toppings. It keeps its texture better than very fresh bread...it's thrifty too!

141

Potato Puff Casserole

Tina George
El Dorado, AR

My family loves this dish served with green beans and dinner rolls.
It's so simple that I'm always happy to fix it for them!

2 lbs. ground beef
10-3/4 oz. can cream of
   mushroom soup
10-3/4 oz. can cream of chicken
   soup

1-1/3 c. milk
6 c. frozen potato puffs
1-1/2 c. shredded Cheddar
   cheese

Brown beef in a skillet over medium heat; drain. Stir in soups and milk; heat through. Transfer to an ungreased 13"x9" baking pan. Layer potato puffs evenly over top. Bake, uncovered, at 375 degrees for 25 minutes, or until puffs are golden. Sprinkle with cheese. Bake an additional 5 minutes, or until cheese is melted. Serves 8.

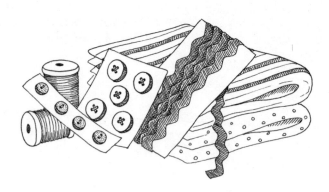

Keep tea towels handy on a peg rack! Stitch a folded
loop of rick rack or twill tape to one corner
of the towels for hanging.

Dinner in a **Dash**

Cornbread-Topped BBQ Beef

Megan Brooks
Antioch, TN

*My sister shared this recipe with me and it has quickly become a
family favorite. Not only is it super-easy to make, it's a good chance
for me to sneak in some veggies for my picky eaters!*

2 lbs. ground beef
1 onion, diced
1 green pepper, diced
11-oz. can corn, drained
14-1/2 oz. can diced tomatoes,
 drained

1/2 c. barbecue sauce
3 8-1/2 oz. pkgs. cornbread
 mix

In a skillet over medium heat, brown beef and onion; drain. Add
vegetables; cook and stir until tender. Stir in sauce; spread mixture in
an ungreased 13"x9" baking pan. Prepare cornbread according to
package directions; spread batter over beef mixture. Bake, uncovered,
at 400 degrees for 20 to 25 minutes, until golden and a knife tip
inserted in the center comes out clean. Serves 8 to 10.

Now and then it's good to pause in our pursuit
of happiness and just be happy.
-Guillaume Apollinaire

Mom's Tuna Patties

Jennifer Baker
Cosby, TN

*This is a great, inexpensive dinner with good flavors...my husband
and children request it often.*

2 eggs, beaten
10-3/4 oz. can cream of
   mushroom soup, divided
3/4 c. milk, divided
2 c. stuffing mix

12-oz. can tuna, drained and
   flaked
1/2 c. shredded Cheddar cheese
2 T. butter

In a bowl, combine eggs, 1/3 of soup and 1/4 cup milk; mix well. Stir
in stuffing mix, tuna and cheese; form into 4 patties. In a skillet over
medium heat, cook patties in butter for 3 to 4 minutes on each side,
until golden and heated through. In a small saucepan over medium
heat, stir together remaining soup and milk until warm. Spoon sauce
over patties. Makes 4 servings.

Comfort foods like tuna patties and creamed chicken
are especially satisfying served over warm split biscuits
or buttered toast...a terrific way to stretch a meal when
there are extra guests for dinner too!

Tangy Beef Patties

Carol Zillig
Lincoln, NE

These tasty little burgers used to be served at our cousins' parties when our children were small. The ingredients in the Special Sauce may seem surprising, but they combine very nicely.

1 c. soft bread crumbs
1/2 c. milk
2 eggs, beaten
2 lbs. ground beef

2 t. salt
1 t. dried, minced onion
1/4 t. pepper

In a large bowl, combine all ingredients and mix together. Form into 10 to 12 silver dollar-size patties. Brown patties in a large skillet over medium heat; drain. Pour Special Sauce over patties and simmer, covered, for 30 minutes. Serves 5 to 6.

Special Sauce:

1 c. chili sauce
3/4 c. grape jelly
1 T. lemon juice

1 t. Worcestershire
1 t. mustard

Mix together ingredients.

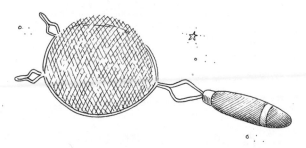

If you're cooking in a skillet and there's no spatter guard handy, a large metal sieve can do the job. Just place it face-down over the skillet.

Angel Hair Italiano

Jo Ann

By the time the pasta pot boils, you're well on the way to a flavorful light meal!

16-oz. pkg. angel hair pasta,
  uncooked
1/4 c. olive oil
4 cloves garlic, pressed
1/2 c. sun-dried tomatoes, finely
  chopped

8-oz. pkg. tomato-basil feta
  cheese, crumbled
1 c. grated Parmesan cheese
1 bunch fresh parsley, chopped
salt and pepper to taste

Cook pasta according to package directions. Drain; return pasta to cooking pot. Mix in oil, garlic, tomatoes and cheeses. Stir in parsley; add salt and pepper to taste. Serve warm. Makes 6 servings.

For a healthy change, give whole-wheat pasta a try
in your favorite pasta recipe...it tastes great and
contains more fiber than regular pasta.

Dinner in a Dash

Garlicky Shrimp & Pasta

Bobbi Scheafnocker
Grove City, PA

My husband and I often use this recipe as our "go-to" dinner when we are out of ideas or short on time and energy.

2 to 3 cloves garlic, minced
5 T. butter
1/2 lb. cooked peeled shrimp, thawed if frozen

cooked angel hair pasta
Garnish: Italian-seasoned dry bread crumbs

In a skillet over medium heat, sauté garlic in butter until just heated through. Add shrimp and heat through. Serve over cooked pasta; garnish with bread crumbs. Makes 2 to 3 servings.

Cook up perfect pasta...here's how! Use 5 quarts of water for each pound of pasta. Bring to a rolling boil over high heat. Stir in pasta; return to a rolling boil. Boil, uncovered, for the time recommended on the package, stirring occasionally to prevent sticking. Drain well before tossing with pasta sauce or a little olive oil.

Quick Chinese One-Dish Meal

Betty Banks
Austin, TX

My hubby thinks this easy-to-make dinner is a great fixer
for the "hungries."

2 T. olive oil
1 cooked chicken breast, cubed
2 c. frozen mixed vegetables,
   thawed

2 c. instant rice, cooked
2 T. light brown sugar, packed
1 t. water
soy sauce to taste

Heat oil in a large skillet over medium-high heat. Add chicken and
cook about 2 to 3 minutes, until hot. Add vegetables and cooked rice.
In a small bowl, mix brown sugar and water together; add to skillet.
Cover skillet; reduce heat to medium and cook until heated through.
Add soy sauce to taste before serving. Makes 6 servings.

It's easy to separate frozen mixed vegetables...place them
in a colander and run under cold water.

Beef & Snow Pea Stir-Fry

Rhonda Reeder
Ellicott City, MD

*My husband and I went to a Chinese restaurant on our first date.
This is my version of the dish he ordered. We have it for our anniversary
every year and it's simply divine!*

3 T. soy sauce
2 T. rice wine or rice vinegar
1 T. brown sugar, packed
1/2 t. cornstarch
1 T. oil
1 T. fresh ginger, minced

1 T. garlic, minced
1 lb. beef round steak, cut into
   thin strips
1 to 1-1/2 c. snow peas
cooked rice

In a small bowl, combine soy sauce, rice wine or vinegar, brown sugar
and cornstarch; set aside. Heat oil in a wok or skillet over medium-
high heat. Add ginger and garlic and sauté for 30 seconds. Add steak
and stir-fry for 2 minutes, or until evenly browned. Add snow peas
and stir-fry for an additional 3 minutes. Add the soy sauce mixture;
bring to a boil, stirring constantly. Reduce heat and simmer until
sauce is thick and smooth. Serve over cooked rice. Makes 4 servings.

After a simple dinner, a sweet & simple dessert is in order.
Place scoops of rainbow sherbet in parfait glasses and
slip a fortune cookie over the edge of each glass...perfect!

Dee's Speedy Skillet Chops

Deanna Lyons
Westerville, OH

*For a quick lunch at **Gooseberry Patch**, I sometimes whip these up for my co-workers and me. Perfect with mashed potatoes!*

1 to 2 T. olive oil
4 boneless pork chops
1/2 t. garlic powder

1 t. paprika
pepper to taste

In a skillet over medium heat, heat oil. Add pork chops and seasonings. Cook for about 10 minutes on each side, until pork chops are cooked through. Makes 2 to 4 servings.

Zesty Zippy Italian Chops

Rita Morgan
Pueblo, CO

This is the quickest, easiest recipe in my recipe box. I make it at least twice a month, especially after the kids' sports events. Great paired with fluffy baked potatoes and green beans.

4 boneless pork chops
1 T. oil
1-1/2 c. zesty Italian salad
   dressing

1 onion, finely chopped
salt and pepper to taste

Brown pork chops in oil in a skillet over medium-high heat, about 3 minutes on both sides. Stir in salad dressing and onion. Cover and cook over medium-low heat for about 25 minutes. Makes 4 servings.

If a favorite non-stick skillet is sticky, fill it with one cup water, 1/2 cup vinegar and 2 tablespoons baking soda. Bring to a boil for a few minutes. Rinse well with hot water, wipe clean and it's good to go!

Dinner in a Dash

Skillet Macaroni & Beef

Jessica Branch
Colchester, IL

This is a nice change from goulash and spaghetti because it all cooks together in the same pan!

1 lb. ground beef
1 t. salt
1 t. pepper
1 t. garlic powder
1/2 c. onion, diced

1/2 c. green pepper, diced
2 8-oz. cans tomato sauce
1 c. water
1-1/2 T. Worcestershire sauce
1 c. elbow macaroni, uncooked

Brown beef in a large skillet over medium heat. Drain; sprinkle with seasonings. Add onion and green pepper; sauté. Add remaining ingredients. Reduce heat; cover and simmer for 20 minutes, stirring occasionally to separate macaroni. Uncover and cook an additional 5 minutes, until thickened. Makes 6 servings.

Make a double batch of your favorite comfort food and invite neighbors over for supper...what a great way to get to know them better. Keep it simple with a tossed salad, warm bakery bread and apple crisp for dessert...it's all about food and fellowship!

Baked Penne & Chicken

Wendy Maryott
Rathdrum, ID

My own version of a dish from our favorite pasta restaurant! Whenever our nieces come for dinner, this is what they ask for.

16-oz. pkg. penne pasta,
   uncooked
2 boneless, skinless chicken
   breasts
seasoned salt to taste

1 t. oil
26-oz. jar spaghetti sauce
16-oz. jar Alfredo sauce
1-1/2 to 2 c. shredded Cheddar
   cheese

Cook pasta according to package directions. While pasta cooks, sprinkle chicken with seasoned salt. In a skillet over medium heat, sauté chicken in oil for about 10 minutes, until cooked through. Set aside to cool. In a stockpot over low heat, combine sauces and heat through, stirring occasionally. Cube chicken and add to sauce mixture. Drain pasta; add to stockpot and toss gently to combine. Pour into an ungreased 13"x9" baking pan and top with cheese. Bake, uncovered, at 350 degrees for 20 minutes, or until cheese is melted and sauce is bubbly. Makes 6 to 8 servings.

Pour vegetable oil into a plastic squeeze bottle.
This makes it easy to drizzle oil just where it's needed,
with no waste and no mess.

3-Cheese Spinach Rigatoni

Audrey Lett
Newark, DE

"Yum" is the word that sums up this recipe. I've gotten so many compliments on this dish...the best part is that it's on the table in less than thirty minutes!

16-oz. pkg. rigatoni pasta,
  uncooked
3 T. olive oil, divided
10-oz. pkg. frozen spinach,
  thawed and drained
2 c. ricotta cheese
5 T. grated Parmesan cheese,
  divided

3/4 t. salt
1/4 t. pepper
Optional: 1/2 t. nutmeg
1-1/2 c. shredded fontina
  cheese, divided
Garnish: additional grated
  Parmesan cheese

Cook rigatoni according to package directions. Drain; toss with one tablespoon oil and place in a greased 13"x9" baking pan. Combine spinach, ricotta and 3 tablespoons Parmesan in a food processor and purée. Add salt, pepper and nutmeg, if desired. Stir in half of fontina; combine spinach mixture with rigatoni. Top with remaining fontina and Parmesan; drizzle with remaining oil. Cover and bake at 450 degrees for 15 to 20 minutes, until golden and heated through. Serve with additional Parmesan cheese for sprinkling. Serves 4.

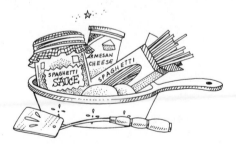

Weekly theme nights make meal planning simple...have family members choose their favorites! They'll look forward to Spaghetti Monday and Tex-Mex Tuesday...you'll always know the answer to "What's for dinner?"

Speedy Tomato Mac & Cheese

Connie Hilty
Pearland, TX

*This is a snap to make and a real family pleaser. My four kids,
ages four to ten, just love it...we never have any leftovers unless
I make a double batch!*

2 c. elbow macaroni, uncooked
10-3/4 oz. can Cheddar cheese
   soup
1 c. zesty spaghetti sauce

1/3 c. milk
Garnish: grated Parmesan
   cheese

Cook macaroni according to package directions; drain and return to
saucepan. Add soup, sauce and milk; mix well and heat through over
medium heat. Serve with Parmesan cheese. Serves 4 to 6.

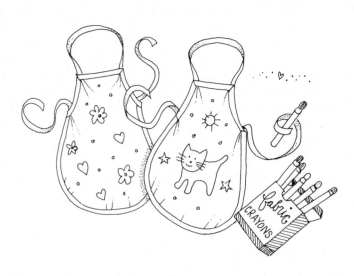

Kids love to "cook" so let them take turns selecting
and helping prepare dinner at least once a week.
It's a great way for them to learn basic kitchen skills.

Dinner in a Dash

Beef & Tomato Gravy

Camille Jones
Long Beach, CA

This recipe was shared with me by my good friend several years ago and I've been making it ever since. It's a very easy midweek meal, very hearty and thrifty too! Delicious with mashed potatoes or rice.

1-1/2 lbs. ground beef
1 onion, minced
1 t. garlic, minced
salt and pepper to taste
1 T. all-purpose flour

2 T. oil
2 14-1/2 oz. cans cut green
   beans, partially drained
28-oz. can diced tomatoes

In a bowl, mix beef with onion, garlic, salt and pepper. Form into 12 silver dollar-size patties. Dredge patties in flour. Heat oil in a large skillet over medium heat; brown patties on both sides. Add green beans and tomatoes with juice; stir to combine. Reduce heat to low. Cover and cook for 20 minutes, stirring once or twice. Serves 6.

Salsa Mac & Cheese

Tammy Steinert
Hoisington, KS

A super meal for hurry-up nights!

7-1/4 oz. pkg. macaroni &
   cheese mix

1/2 lb. ground beef, browned
1/2 c. salsa

Prepare macaroni & cheese according to package directions. Add beef and salsa to same saucepan. Stir well and heat through over low heat. Serves 4.

Better with Bacon Noodles

Sherry Gordon
Arlington Heights, IL

This casserole recipe was handed down to me by my Hungarian grandmother. It was already a good recipe, but I tossed in a little bacon, and what do you know? It made this yummy traditional dish even yummier.

16-oz. pkg. wide egg noodles,
   cooked
2 c. sour cream
12-oz. container cottage cheese

3-1/2 slices smoked bacon,
   crisply cooked and crumbled
salt and pepper to taste

In a lightly greased 13"x9" baking pan, blend together cooked noodles and sour cream. Spoon cottage cheese evenly over noodle mixture. Sprinkle crumbled bacon on top. Add salt and pepper to taste. Bake, uncovered, at 350 degrees for about 15 minutes, until heated through and cheese softens. Serves 8.

Add some fresh broccoli, asparagus or snow peas to a favorite pasta recipe...simply drop chopped veggies into the pasta pot about halfway through the cooking time. Pasta and veggies will be tender at about the same time.

Dinner in a Dash

Pepper Bacon-Tomato Linguine
Virginia Watson
Scranton, PA

*Just minutes from start to finish, and so incredibly good,
you'll feel you've treated yourself and your family to a nice dinner
at a fancy restaurant!*

16-oz. pkg. linguine pasta, uncooked
1/2 lb. peppered bacon, diced
2 T. green onions, chopped
2 t. garlic, minced

14-1/2 oz. can diced tomatoes
1 t. dried basil
salt and pepper to taste
3 T. grated Parmesan cheese

Cook pasta according to package directions; drain. Meanwhile, in a large skillet over medium heat, cook bacon until crisp. Remove bacon to a paper towel; reserve drippings in skillet. Add onion and garlic to drippings; sauté for one minute. Stir in tomatoes with juice and seasonings; simmer for 5 minutes. Add linguine, Parmesan cheese and bacon; toss to mix well. Serves 6.

Make a fresh-tasting side dish. Combine 3 to 4 sliced zucchini, 1/2 teaspoon minced garlic and a tablespoon of chopped fresh basil. Sauté in a little olive oil until tender and serve warm.

Ralph Ratliff's Chicken

Kellie Trail-Wells
Christiansburg, VA

Growing up, one of my favorite things was the potluck lunches at our church. I loved the delicious smells, the excitement of the adults getting food prepared and the children playing. I always put way more food on my plate than I could eat, but how could I resist such tempting dishes? My favorite was a chicken casserole made by a church member named Ralph Ratliff. Eventually Mom asked him for the recipe and many years later, it's still a favorite...comfort food based on memories of a sweet time.

3 to 4 c. cooked chicken, cubed
10-3/4 oz. can chicken noodle
   soup
10-3/4 oz. can cream of
   mushroom soup
1 egg, beaten

3 slices bread, cubed
1 sleeve round buttery crackers,
   crumbled
1/4 c. butter, melted
1/4 c. shredded Colby cheese

In a bowl, mix together chicken, soups, egg and bread cubes. Pour mixture into a greased 13"x9" baking pan. Toss together cracker crumbs and butter; sprinkle over top. Sprinkle cheese over crumb mixture. Bake, uncovered, at 350 degrees for about 30 minutes, until hot and bubbly. Makes 4 to 6 servings.

Stock up on favorite pantry items when they're on sale...they're oh-so handy for homestyle meals in a hurry. Write the purchase date on the package with a permanent marker to make cupboard rotation easy.

Pepper Chicken

Tracey Regnold
Lewisville, TX

*This was my mother's recipe and I have modified it to fit our family.
It's a favorite at our house. This dish can be made with beef too.*

1 onion, chopped
1 green pepper, chopped
1 to 2 cloves garlic, chopped
2 to 3 T. olive oil
4 boneless, skinless chicken
    breasts, cubed
1/2 to 3/4 c. white wine or
    chicken broth

10-3/4 oz. can cream of
    mushroom soup
10-3/4 oz. can golden
    mushroom soup
1/2 c. chicken broth
salt and pepper to taste
cooked rice or egg noodles

In a skillet over medium heat, sauté onion, green pepper and garlic in
oil until onion is translucent, 2 to 3 minutes. Add chicken and cook
until golden, about 3 to 4 minutes; drain. Add wine or broth and cook
for one to 2 minutes. Add soups, broth, salt and pepper, stirring well
to combine. Simmer, over medium-low heat for about 10 minutes.
Serve over hot cooked rice or noodles. Makes 4 to 5 servings.

Keep your wooden cutting board in tip-top shape. Protect it
from spills by coating with a thin film of olive oil and
letting it soak in for a few minutes. Rub dry with a paper
towel; repeat several times. Let the board stand for
24 hours before using again.

Delia's Shortcut Paella

Delia Chiu
Columbia, MD

*I admit I don't really know what goes into an authentic Spanish paella!
However, I recently discovered a really tasty Spanish rice in the frozen
foods section of the supermarket. By adding a few simple ingredients, I
created a quick and delicious one-pot meal!*

12-oz. pkg. frozen Spanish rice
1/4 c. pine nuts
1 T. oil
1/2 c. sweet onion, chopped

1 c. cooked chicken strips
1/2 c. cherry tomatoes, halved
Optional: fresh parsley, chopped

Microwave Spanish rice according to package instructions; set aside.
In a skillet over low heat, toast pine nuts; remove and set aside. Add
oil and onion to skillet; sauté over medium heat. Add chicken and
tomatoes; heat through. Add Spanish rice to skillet; cook and stir for
several minutes. Stir in pine nuts. Garnish with parsley, if desired.
Serves 4.

Frozen packages of chopped onion, cut-up green peppers
and stir-fry vegetables can take minutes off mealtime
preparations...no chopping, mincing or dicing!

Dinner in a Dash

Spicy Black Beans & Quinoa

Rita Morgan
Pueblo, CO

*I'm the only vegetarian in my family, but my husband and teenage son
love this dish as much as I do. I usually serve it with warm
cornbread and a Southwestern salad. So yummy!*

1 t. oil
1 onion, chopped
3 cloves garlic, chopped
3/4 c. quinoa, uncooked
1-1/2 c. vegetable broth
1 t. ground cumin

1/4 t. cayenne pepper
salt and pepper to taste
1 c. frozen corn
2 15-oz. cans black beans,
   drained and rinsed
1/2 c. fresh cilantro, chopped

Heat oil in a saucepan over medium heat; sauté onion and garlic until
golden. Stir in quinoa, broth and seasonings; bring mixture to a boil.
Reduce heat; cover and simmer for 20 minutes. Stir in corn and
beans; cook an additional 5 minutes, or until heated through. Mix in
cilantro. Makes 8 to 10 servings.

Serve almost-instant herbed butter with warm rolls tonight!
Press a mixture of dried oregano, thyme, parsley and a dash
of garlic powder over a stick of chilled butter and slice.

Meatball Cream Stew

Yoshiko Davis
Olathe, KS

*This made-from-scratch recipe may look a little complicated,
but it goes together quickly...and the flavor is well worth it!*

1 lb. ground pork
1 t. garlic paste or 1/8 t. garlic
   powder
1 c. dry bread crumbs
2 eggs, beaten
1/2 t. salt
1/4 t. pepper
6 c. water
3 cubes chicken bouillon

1/4 c. white wine or chicken
   broth
1 bay leaf
1 onion, thinly sliced
12 Brussels sprouts, trimmed
2 potatoes, peeled and cubed
1-1/2 c. whipping cream
1/4 c. butter
1/4 c. all-purpose flour

Combine pork, garlic paste or powder, bread crumbs, eggs, salt and
pepper in a bowl. Mix well; form into one-inch balls and set aside. In
a heavy stockpot over medium-high heat, bring water, bouillon cubes,
wine or broth and bay leaf to a boil. Add meatballs and cook for
10 minutes. Add onion, Brussels sprouts and potatoes; cook for an
additional 10 minutes. Stir in cream; bring to a boil. Blend butter and
flour together to form a paste; add to stew. Cook and stir until heated
through and slightly thickened. Discard bay leaf. Serves 6.

Trying to cut down on salt? Choose low-sodium canned
soups, broth and veggies...experiment with fresh chopped
herbs for extra flavor. You can also use garlic powder
instead of garlic salt. Just taste and adjust seasonings
when the dish has finished cooking.

Dinner in a Dash

Girl "Stout" Stew

Anne Tarver
Dawsonville, GA

We always made this stew over the Girl Scout campfire when I was growing up. Years later I would make it for my family. My son loved it but always pronounced it Girl "Stout" Stew...so "Stout" it is! Just add some crackers and serve with fruit. Quick, easy and very good!

1 lb. ground beef
1 onion, chopped
10-3/4 oz. can vegetarian
    vegetable soup

1 c. water
salt and pepper to taste

In a large saucepan over medium heat, cook beef and onion until beef is no longer pink. Drain; stir in remaining ingredients. Reduce heat and simmer for 15 minutes. Makes 4 servings.

Just for fun, serve up soft pretzels instead of dinner rolls.
Twist strips of refrigerated bread stick dough into
pretzel shapes and place on an ungreased baking sheet.
Brush with beaten egg white, sprinkle with coarse
salt and bake as directed.

Broccoli-Chicken Casserole

Gladys Brehm
Quakertown, PA

This hearty one-dish dinner goes together oh-so quickly! It's a tasty way to turn leftover chicken into a second meal.

10-3/4 oz. can cream of
   mushroom soup
1-1/2 c. milk
6-oz. pkg. chicken-flavored
   stuffing mix
3 c. cooked chicken, cubed

10-oz. pkg. frozen chopped
   broccoli, thawed
1 onion, finely chopped
2 stalks celery, finely chopped
Optional: 1/2 c. shredded
   mozzarella cheese

Whisk soup and milk together in a large bowl. Stir in remaining ingredients except cheese; mix well. Transfer to a 3-quart casserole dish that has been sprayed with non-stick vegetable spray. Bake, uncovered, at 350 degrees for 35 to 40 minutes. If desired, sprinkle with cheese during the last 10 minutes of baking time. Serves 4 to 6.

Unsure about the capacity of a favorite casserole dish...two quarts or three? Just measure out water, one quart at a time, and pour into the dish to check.

Dinner in a
Dash

Momma Rita's Quick Casserole
Rita Bomberry
Desoto, MO

*Being a busy mom of six kids, I invented this one-pot meal.
Of course the kids love it, since it has lots of cheese in it!*

1 lb. ground turkey
1/4 onion, diced
garlic powder and pepper
   to taste
2 14-1/2 oz. cans green beans,
   drained

2 15-1/4 oz. cans corn, drained
2 15-oz. cans diced potatoes,
   drained
seasoned salt to taste
5 to 10 slices American cheese

Brown turkey with onion in a large stockpot over medium heat;
drain. Add garlic powder and pepper to taste. Stir in green beans,
corn and potatoes; add seasoned salt to taste. Heat through, stirring
occasionally. Top with cheese slices as desired. Simmer over low heat
about 10 minutes, until cheese is melted. Stir to combine. Serves 6.

Tie ruffled vintage aprons onto the backs of kitchen chairs
for a sweet welcome to a country-style supper.

Parmesan Pork Chops

Amy Wrightsel
Louisville, KY

A must-have easy Friday night meal that's ready in minutes!

1/4 c. butter, melted
1/4 c. grated Parmesan cheese
2 T. all-purpose flour
2 t. Italian seasoning

2 t. dried parsley
1/4 t. pepper
8 boneless pork chops
1/4 c. oil

Place melted butter in a shallow bowl. Combine remaining ingredients except pork chops and oil in a separate shallow bowl. Dip pork chops in butter, then coat in Parmesan mixture. In a large skillet over medium heat, cook pork chops in oil until golden and no longer pink, about 3 minutes on each side. Makes 8 servings.

Turn a packaged wild rice mix into your own special blend in a jiffy. Sauté a cup of chopped mushrooms, onion and celery in butter until tender...you can even toss in some dried cranberries or raisins. Add the rice mix and prepare as the package directs.

Dinner in a Dash

Super-Fast Tilapia Parmesan

Kendall Hale
Lynn, MA

So quick, delicious and good for you too. You'll want to make this recipe again and again!

1/2 c. grated Parmesan cheese
1/4 c. butter, softened
3 T. mayonnaise
2 T. lemon juice
1/4 t. dried basil

1/4 t. pepper
1/8 t. onion powder
1/8 t. celery salt
2 lbs. tilapia fillets

In a small bowl, blend together all ingredients except fish fillets; set aside. Arrange fillets in a single layer on a lightly greased broiler pan. Broil on top rack of oven for 2 to 3 minutes. Turn and broil other side for 2 to 3 minutes. Remove from oven; cover fish with Parmesan mixture. Broil for 2 additional minutes, or until topping is golden and fish flakes easily with a fork. Makes 8 servings.

A crisp green salad goes well with all kinds of main dishes. For a zippy homemade lemon dressing, shake up 1/2 cup olive oil, 1/3 cup fresh lemon juice and a tablespoon of Dijon mustard in a small jar and chill to blend.

Garden Skillet Dinner with Chicken

Jennie Gist
Gooseberry Patch

This is one-pot comfort food at its finest...warm chicken and vegetables over noodles. Plus, clean-up is quick as a wink!

1 lb. boneless skinless chicken breast, diced
1/4 c. all-purpose flour
1/3 c. olive oil
2 T. garlic, minced
1/2 c. red pepper, sliced
1/2 c. carrot, peeled and sliced

1/2 c. celery, sliced
1/2 c. broccoli flowerets
1 T. dried basil
3/4 c. chicken broth
3/4 c. whipping cream
12-oz. pkg. egg noodles, cooked
salt and pepper to taste

Combine chicken and flour in a large plastic zipping bag. Shake until chicken is evenly coated; discard remaining flour. Heat oil in a large skillet over medium heat. Sauté chicken in oil until golden and no longer pink in the center. Add garlic, vegetables and basil; cook for 2 minutes. Reduce heat to low; stir in broth and cream. When mixture has thickened slightly, stir in noodles. Heat through; season with salt and pepper. Serves 4 to 6.

Tasty Turkey Roll-Ups

Tammy Rowe
Bellevue, OH

My kids love these! I use this recipe whenever I have extra lunchmeat left at the end of the week that I need to use up quickly.

6-oz. pkg. stuffing mix
1 lb. deli turkey, thickly sliced
2/3 c. milk

10-3/4 oz. can cream of chicken soup

Prepare stuffing mix according to package directions. Spoon an even amount in the center of each turkey slice. Roll up; place seam-down in a greased 13"x9" baking pan. Mix together milk and soup; spoon over roll-ups. Cover; bake at 350 degrees for 30 minutes. Serves 4.

Dinner in a Dash

Hamburger Stroganoff

Tina Wright
White House, TN

*So creamy and satisfying...real comfort food! My mother
shared this tried & true recipe with me.*

1-1/2 lbs. ground beef
1 onion, chopped
1 to 2 t. garlic, minced
10-3/4 oz. can cream of
   mushroom soup
10-3/4 oz. can cream of chicken
   soup

1-1/2 c. sour cream
pepper to taste
16-oz. pkg. sliced mushrooms
2 T. butter
cooked wide egg noodles
Garnish: shredded Parmesan
   cheese

Brown beef in a large skillet over medium heat. Add onion and garlic;
cook until onion is translucent. Stir in soups; reduce heat and simmer
for 10 to 15 minutes. Stir in sour cream and pepper; simmer an
additional 5 minutes. Meanwhile, in a separate skillet over medium
heat, sauté mushrooms in butter until tender, about 3 to 4 minutes.
Gently mix beef mixture and mushrooms with cooked noodles.
Garnish with cheese. Makes 6 servings.

Keep favorite busy-day
recipes right at your
fingertips...store them
in a vintage
tin lunchbox.

Stuffed Artichoke Chicken

Michelle Marckesano
East Meadow, NY

One of my husband's favorite meals. The filling was originally served as an appetizer...one day I decided to try filling chicken cutlets with it and it was a big hit!

1 c. mayonnaise
1 onion, chopped
1 c. grated Parmesan cheese
14-oz. can artichoke hearts,
 drained and chopped
1 T. lemon juice

1/2 t. pepper
2 lbs. boneless chicken cutlets
salt and pepper to taste
3 T. olive oil
3/4 c. seasoned dry bread
 crumbs

Combine mayonnaise, onion, cheese, artichokes, lemon juice and pepper in a bowl; set aside. Flatten chicken cutlets between 2 pieces of wax paper until thin; sprinkle with salt and pepper. Spread artichoke mixture onto each chicken cutlet. Roll up; secure with a wooden toothpick. Drizzle roll-ups with oil; coat with bread crumbs. Place in an ungreased 13"x9" baking pan. Bake, uncovered, at 350 degrees for 30 minutes. Makes 8 servings.

Looking for a new family message board? Hang an old-fashioned washboard for a whimsical way to keep notes organized. Hot-glue magnets to old-fashioned wooden clip clothespins to hold notes and photos in place.

Dinner in a
Dash

Dijon Company Chicken

Tori Willis
Champaign, IL

I serve this elegant dish when we're having friends for dinner but don't have a lot of time. The chicken is so tender it practically melts in your mouth!

4 boneless, skinless chicken
   breasts
1/4 c. Dijon mustard
1/4 c. evaporated milk

1/4 c. dry bread crumbs
1/4 c. grated Parmesan cheese
2 T. olive oil

Flatten chicken breasts between 2 pieces of wax paper until thin; set aside. Combine mustard and evaporated milk in a shallow bowl. Combine bread crumbs and cheese in a separate shallow bowl. Dip chicken into mustard mixture, then into bread crumb mixture, coating both sides. Heat oil in a skillet over medium-high heat; brown chicken for about 3 minutes on each side. Arrange chicken in a lightly greased 9"x9" baking pan. Bake, uncovered, at 400 degrees for 20 to 25 minutes, until chicken is golden and no longer pink in the center. Makes 4 servings.

Set out a guest book when friends come to dinner! Ask everyone young and old to sign...it will become a treasured memento. Add notes about the menu and everyone's likes & dislikes to simplify future meal planning.

Speedy Pizza Bake

*Charlotte Smith
Tyrone, PA*

*Yummy, fast and so easy you can let the kids take over! Add extra
toppings like olives, peppers and onions, if you like.*

2 7-oz. pkgs. biscuit baking
 mix
1 c. water
14-oz. jar pizza sauce, divided

4-oz. pkg. sliced pepperoni,
 divided
2 c. shredded mozzarella cheese,
 divided

In a bowl, stir together biscuit mix and water until a soft dough forms.
Spray a 13"x9" glass baking pan with non-stick vegetable spray. Drop
half of dough by spoonfuls evenly into bottom of baking pan; dough
will not completely cover bottom of pan. Drizzle one cup pizza sauce
over dough. Arrange 1/2 of pepperoni slices evenly over sauce. Top
with one cup cheese. Repeat layering. Bake, uncovered, at 375 degrees
for 20 to 25 minutes, until golden. Cut into squares. Serves 6.

To grate or shred a block of cheese easily, place the
wrapped cheese in the freezer for 10 to 20 minutes...it will
just glide across the grater!

172

Dinner in a Dash

Pizzeria Sausage Supper

Kay Jones
Cleburne, TX

My children loved pizza when they were growing up, like most kids do. When I came across this recipe, I added my own touches and they loved it because it had all their favorite pizza flavors. Add a salad and you've got a meal!

1 lb. ground pork sausage
1/2 c. onion, chopped
1/4 c. green pepper, chopped
2 T. all-purpose flour
16-oz. can diced tomatoes
4-oz. can mushroom stems & pieces, drained
1 t. fresh oregano, chopped
1/2 t. fresh basil, chopped

1/4 t. garlic powder
1/8 t. pepper
Optional: 4-oz. pkg. sliced pepperoni
10-oz. tube refrigerated biscuits, quartered
2 c. shredded mozzarella cheese
Optional: grated Parmesan cheese

In a large ovenproof skillet over medium heat, brown sausage, onion and pepper. Drain; sprinkle with flour. Add undrained tomatoes, mushrooms and seasonings; mix well. Simmer until hot and bubbly, stirring until slightly thickened. Add pepperoni, if desired. Arrange biscuit quarters over mixture in skillet. Sprinkle biscuit layer with mozzarella cheese. Bake, uncovered, at 400 degrees for 12 to 16 minutes, until biscuits are golden. Garnish with Parmesan, if desired. Makes about 10 servings.

When freezing leftover diced peppers, corn or fresh herbs, add a little olive oil to the plastic zipping bag and shake. The oil will help keep the food separate and fresher too...all ready to drop into sauces and salsas!

All-in-One Supper

Lynn Knepp
Montgomery, IN

This is my tried & true recipe when our Florida relatives visit or when I'm taking a dish to share with neighbors. It's mmm good! The secret to the wonderful taste is the seared sausage in the bottom of the pan. For a little different flavor, add some cabbage or corn.

1-lb. smoked pork sausage ring, sliced diagonally
2 14-1/2 oz. cans green beans, drained

4 potatoes, peeled and cubed
Optional: 1/2 c. onion, chopped
salt and pepper to taste

In a skillet over high heat, brown the sausage quickly, stirring often. Add green beans, potatoes and onion if using. Add enough water to cover bottom of skillet; sprinkle with salt and pepper. Reduce heat to low; simmer, uncovered, for 30 minutes. Makes 6 servings.

A pretty china saucer that has lost its teacup can still be useful. Place it beside the stovetop to serve as a spoon rest.

Dinner in a Dash

Big Daddy's Beefy Mac

Joshua Logan
Corpus Christi, TX

Whenever my wife is out for the evening, Big Daddy's Beefy Mac is what's for dinner. I'm no expert chef, but as my kids will tell you, I like to eat a lot...and this recipe is really good!

3/4 lb. ground beef
14-oz. can vegetable broth
8-oz. can stewed tomatoes
1 T. Worcestershire sauce
1/2 t. dried oregano
1/2 t. garlic powder
1-1/2 c. elbow macaroni, uncooked
salt and pepper to taste
Optional: 1 t. red pepper flakes

Brown beef in a large skillet over medium-high heat. Drain; add broth, tomatoes with juice, Worcestershire sauce and seasonings. Bring to a boil; stir in uncooked macaroni. Season with salt, pepper and red pepper flakes, if desired. Cover and cook over medium heat for 10 minutes, stirring often. Uncover; cook an additional 5 minutes, or until macaroni is tender. Serves 4.

Mount a wrought-iron curtain rod over the stove, then use S-hooks to hang up pots and pans...so convenient!

Make-Ahead Chicken-Chile Rolls *Angela Murphy*
Tempe, AZ

Make this scrumptious casserole the night before, refrigerate it overnight and pop it in the oven the next evening...what a timesaver!

6 boneless, skinless chicken
   breasts
1/4 lb. Monterey Jack cheese,
   cut into 6 strips
7-oz. jar diced chiles, divided
1/2 c. dry bread crumbs
1/2 c. grated Parmesan cheese
1 T. chili powder

1/2 t. salt
1/4 t. pepper
1/4 t. ground cumin
1/4 c. plus 2 T. butter, melted
2 c. enchilada sauce
Garnish: shredded Mexican-
   blend cheese, sour cream,
   diced tomatoes, green onions

Flatten chicken breasts to 1/4-inch thin between pieces of wax paper. Top each piece of chicken with one strip of cheese and 2 tablespoons chiles; roll up. Combine bread crumbs, Parmesan cheese and seasonings in a bowl; place melted butter in a separate bowl. Dip chicken rolls in butter and coat in crumb mixture. Arrange chicken rolls in a lightly greased 13"x9" baking pan, seam-side down; drizzle with any remaining butter. Cover and chill overnight. The next day, uncover and bake at 400 degrees for 30 minutes, until heated through. Shortly before serving time, warm enchilada sauce in a saucepan or in the microwave; ladle sauce evenly over chicken. Garnish as desired. Serves 6.

Pick up a dozen pint-size Mason jars...perfect for serving cold beverages at casual get-togethers with family & friends.

Dinner in a ⟩⟩⟩⟩⟩⟩
Dash

Renae's Taco Casserole

Renae Scheiderer
Beallsville, OH

This recipe was shared with me the first Christmas after I was married. It's become a favorite quick & easy supper at our house!

1 lb. ground beef
1-1/4 oz. pkg. taco seasoning
  mix
15-oz. can tomato sauce
3 c. elbow macaroni, cooked

8-oz. container sour cream
1 c. shredded Cheddar cheese,
  divided
1/4 c. grated Parmesan cheese

In a skillet over medium heat, brown beef. Drain; stir in seasoning mix and tomato sauce. Bring to a boil and remove from heat. In a bowl, combine cooked macaroni, sour cream and 1/2 cup Cheddar cheese. Spoon macaroni mixture into a lightly greased 13"x9" baking pan. Top with beef mixture and remaining cheeses. Bake, uncovered, at 350 degrees for 30 minutes, until hot and bubbly. Serves 6.

Keep the cupboard tidy...tuck packets of salad and seasoning mix into a vintage napkin holder.

On-the-Run Chicken Pot Pie

Charlene McCain
Bakersfield, CA

A terrific recipe for those nights when you want a nutritious, homestyle meal for your family but don't have a lot of time.

2 potatoes, peeled and diced
2 carrots, peeled and chopped
1 onion, diced
2 stalks celery, chopped
1 c. water, divided
10-3/4 oz. can cream of chicken
    soup
1/2 c. milk

1 to 1-1/2 c. cooked chicken,
    diced
salt and pepper to taste
1/2 c. frozen peas
9-inch pie crust, cut into 1-inch
    wide strips
1 egg, beaten

Place potatoes, carrots, onion, celery and 1/2 cup water in a microwave-safe bowl. Cover and microwave on high for 15 minutes. Meanwhile, heat soup with milk and remaining water in a saucepan over medium heat; stir in chicken, salt and pepper. When vegetables are done, drain and place in an ungreased 2-quart casserole dish. Add peas; spoon chicken mixture into dish. Arrange pie crust strips on top lattice-style; brush with egg. Bake at 425 degrees for 15 to 20 minutes, until crust is golden and mixture is hot and bubbly. Serves 4.

An intricate woven lattice pie crust is glorious, but there's an easier way! Simply lay half the strips of crust across the pie filling in one direction, then lay the remaining strips at right angles...and it's done!

Dinner in a Dash

Un-Stuffed Peppers

Diana Spray
Medora, IN

One of my husband's favorite meals...this tastes like stuffed peppers, but it's so much easier. We raise our own green peppers and freeze them, and we also can our own tomatoes, so we fix this a lot in late summer with garden-fresh produce. Yum!

1 lb. ground beef
2 c. green peppers, sliced
8-oz. jar pasteurized process
   cheese sauce
1 c. instant rice, cooked

1 c. tomato, chopped
1/4 c. onion, diced
1/8 t. dried basil
1/8 t. pepper

Brown meat and peppers in a skillet over medium heat; drain. Reduce heat and continue cooking for 5 minutes, or until peppers are crisp-tender. Add remaining ingredients and heat through. Makes 4 servings.

A quick & tasty side for any south-of-the-border main dish...stir spicy salsa and shredded cheese into hot cooked instant rice. Cover and let stand a few minutes, until cheese melts.

Pork & Noodle Stir-Fry

Jean Fuentes
Las Vegas, NV

My family loves this recipe, and it is so easy to prepare! It's great if I don't really feel like cooking when I get home. Sometimes I'll pass the spaghetti separately at the table or serve with speedy instant rice. Boneless chicken and beef are delicious too.

8-oz. pkg. thin spaghetti, uncooked
1 T. oil
1 lb. boneless pork chops, cut into bite-size pieces

garlic powder and salt to taste
soy sauce to taste
16-oz. pkg. frozen stir-fry vegetables

Cook spaghetti according to package directions; drain. Meanwhile, heat oil in a large stir-fry pan or skillet over medium-high heat. Add pork, seasonings and soy sauce. Increase heat to high. Cook until pork is almost done, stirring frequently, about 10 minutes. Add frozen vegetables and cook until tender. Add cooked spaghetti to pan. Stir-fry for just a few minutes until all ingredients are tossed together well, adding more soy sauce if desired while stirring. Makes 6 to 8 servings.

Quick-cooking thin spaghetti, ramen noodles and instant rice can become the basis for all kinds of homestyle-in-a-hurry dishes. They're handy for stretching a dish for extra guests too.

Dinner in a
Dash

Crumb-Topped Baked Haddock
Tammy Munn
Watertown, NY

Such an easy way to prepare fish fillets!

1-1/2 lbs. haddock fillets
2 to 3 T. mayonnaise
1-1/4 c. cracker crumbs

3 to 4 T. butter, melted
salt and pepper to taste
paprika to taste

Place fish fillets in a shallow baking pan that has been sprayed with non-stick vegetable spray. Spread mayonnaise over fish. Toss together cracker crumbs, butter, salt and pepper; sprinkle evenly over fish. Sprinkle with a little paprika. Cover and bake at 400 degrees for 10 to 15 minutes, until fish flakes easily. Serves 4 to 6.

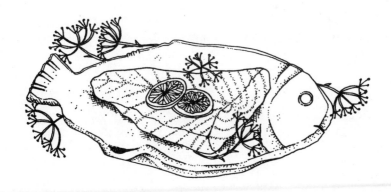

A handy tip to make frozen fish taste fresh and mild! Place the frozen fillets in a shallow dish, cover with milk and place them in the refrigerator to thaw overnight.

Chicken Nuggets Parmesan

Jenny Bishoff
Swanton, MD

I have two preschoolers and a full-time job, so this easy casserole is a real time-saver! Serve with cooked spaghetti, if you like.

13-1/2 oz. pkg. frozen chicken
   nuggets
1/2 c. grated Parmesan cheese

26-1/2 oz. jar spaghetti sauce
1 c. shredded mozzarella cheese
1 t. Italian seasoning

Arrange chicken nuggets in an 11"x7" baking pan sprayed with non-stick vegetable spray. Top with remaining ingredients in order given. Cover with aluminum foil; bake at 350 degrees for 30 minutes. Serves 4 to 6.

Simple Garlic Chicken

Zoe Bennett
Columbia, SC

Just five ingredients and twenty minutes from start to finish...you just can't go wrong with this recipe! It's really delicious served with rice and a crisp garden salad.

3 T. butter
4 boneless, skinless chicken
   breasts

2 t. garlic powder
1 t. onion powder
1 t. seasoned salt

Melt butter in a large skillet over medium-high heat. Add chicken and sprinkle with seasonings. Sauté about 10 to 15 minutes on each side, until chicken is cooked through and juices run clear. Serves 4.

Easy-as-Pie Desserts

Brown Sugar Cake

Cindy Lyzenga
Zeeland, MI

This cake is easy and fun to make! It is always a hit at our church potlucks and I never take home any leftovers.

18-1/2 oz. pkg. white cake mix
3.4-oz. pkg. instant vanilla
   pudding mix
2 eggs, beaten

2 c. milk
3/4 c. brown sugar, packed
3/4 c. semi-sweet chocolate
   chips

In a large bowl, stir together dry cake and pudding mixes, eggs and milk. Pour batter into a greased 13"x9" baking pan. Sprinkle brown sugar and chocolate chips over batter. Bake at 375 degrees for 30 to 35 minutes, until cake tests done. Makes 12 servings.

When time is short, a super-fast dessert is in order.
Layer cubes of angel food cake with cherry or blueberry
pie filling in pretty parfait glasses. Add a dollop of
whipped topping...yummy!

Easy-as-Pie Desserts

Hasty Peach Cobbler

Cynthia Green
Worthington, IN

*This recipe is a lifesaver when you have last-minute dinner guests.
Mix it up quick, pop it in the oven and by the time you've finished
dinner, a scrumptious warm dessert is ready. Try it with other flavors
of pie filling too.*

1/2 c. all-purpose flour
1/2 c. sugar
1 t. baking powder
1/2 c. milk

2 T. butter, diced
21-oz. can peach pie filling
Garnish: vanilla ice cream

In a bowl, mix together flour, sugar and baking powder. Add milk and
stir to mix well. Dot a 9"x9" baking pan with butter; pour batter into
pan. Spoon peaches over batter. Bake at 375 degrees for 30 minutes,
until golden. Serve warm, topped with a scoop of ice cream. Makes
6 servings.

Forget about anything fussy...enjoy dessert outside
and let the crumbs fall where they may!

Berry Cream Tarts

Diana Chaney
Olathe, KS

*These cream-filled tarts look like you went to a lot of effort,
but they're a snap to make. A luscious way to serve dewy-fresh
berries from the farmers' market!*

10-oz. pkg. frozen puff pastry
   shells, thawed
1/4 c. milk
1/4 c. brown sugar, packed
8-oz. pkg. cream cheese,
   softened

1/2 c. sugar
1/2 t. cinnamon
1-1/2 c. favorite berries
Optional: whipped topping

Place pastry shells on a lightly greased baking sheet. Brush shells
with milk and sprinkle with brown sugar. Bake at 375 degrees for
10 to 15 minutes, until shells turn golden. Remove from oven and
remove tops of shells; set aside. In a bowl, blend together cream
cheese, sugar and cinnamon. Spoon 2 tablespoons of cream cheese
mixture into each shell; top with berries. Replace tops. Return filled
shells to oven and bake an additional 5 minutes, or until filling is
warm and bubbly and tops are golden. Garnish with whipped topping,
if desired. Makes one dozen.

Use a sugar shaker to
save clean-up time in the
kitchen...it's ideal for dusting
powdered sugar onto desserts
warm from the oven.

Easy-as-Pie Desserts

Speedy Little Devils

Dolores Brown
Martinsburg, WV

When my son was a junior in high school, he tried these bars at a friend's house. The friend's mom sent the recipe home with my son and he told me I had to make some too. He just turned forty recently and I'm still making these yummy bars for him!

18-1/4 oz. pkg. devil's food
  cake mix
1/2 c. butter, softened

1 c. creamy peanut butter
13-oz. jar marshmallow creme

Blend together dry cake mix and butter; reserve one cup of mixture for topping. Place remaining mixture in an ungreased 8"x8" baking pan; press to form a crust. Blend together peanut butter and marshmallow creme; carefully spread across crust. Sprinkle with reserved topping. Bake at 350 degrees for 20 minutes, until lightly golden. Do not overbake as bars will become too hard. Cool; cut into bars. Makes one dozen.

A pizza cutter is handy for cutting brownies and bar cookies neatly. Dip the cutter into warm water between cuts.

187

Easy Angel Food Bars

Becky Holsinger
Reedsville, OH

When I need a quick & easy dessert, I make these bars. As yummy as they are, people think they took a lot longer to make! Pineapple is my favorite, but you can use any kind of pie filling.

16-oz. pkg. angel food cake mix   21-oz. can pineapple pie filling

Combine dry cake mix and pie filling; blend until smooth. Pour batter into an ungreased 15"x10" jelly-roll pan. Bake at 350 degrees for 20 to 25 minutes, until golden and top springs back when lightly touched. Cool in pan; cut into squares. Makes 2 dozen.

For buffets or dinner parties, roll up flatware ahead of time in colorful napkins and stack in a basket...or let the kids do it for you!

Easy-as-Pie Desserts

Sweet Apple Dumplings

Becca Jones
Jackson, TN

This recipe is a family favorite and has been used often for special occasions as well as weekday suppers. It is very easy to prepare. I hope you enjoy it as much as we do!

2 Granny Smith apples, cored, peeled and quartered
cinnamon to taste
8-oz. tube refrigerated crescent rolls

1/2 c. butter, melted
1 c. orange juice
1 c. sugar
Garnish: vanilla ice cream or whipped topping

Toss apple quarters with cinnamon; set aside. Separate crescent rolls; wrap each apple quarter in a roll. Arrange in a 13"x9" baking pan sprayed with non-stick vegetable spray. Mix together butter, orange juice and sugar; blend well. Drizzle over wrapped apples. Bake at 350 degrees for 28 to 30 minutes, or until golden and apples are tender. Serve warm, garnished as desired. Makes 8 servings.

Keep a shaker jar of apple pie spice handy if you love to bake. A blend of cinnamon, nutmeg and allspice, it's scrumptious in all kinds of baked goods, from pies to cookies to quick breads.

Grandmother's Apple Crunch

Karen Sylvia
Brighton, CO

*My sons love this yummy old-fashioned dessert! My grandmother
used to make this delicious recipe in the fall and it has been
handed down for two generations.*

6 to 8 Granny Smith apples,
   cored, peeled and sliced
1/2 c. brown sugar, packed
1/2 c. sugar

1/2 c. all-purpose flour
1/2 c. butter, softened
cinnamon to taste
Optional: vanilla ice cream

Place apples in an ungreased 8"x8" baking pan; set aside. In a bowl,
mix remaining ingredients except ice cream. Sprinkle mixture over
apples. Bake at 350 degrees for 30 minutes, or until apples are tender.
Serve warm, topped with ice cream, if desired. Serves 6.

Keep a spray mister full of lemon juice in the fridge. So
handy for spritzing sliced pears, apples or peaches...adds
extra zing and prevents browning too!

Easy-as-Pie
Desserts

Speedy White Chocolate Fudge

Vicki Echols
Corydon, KY

Made in the microwave...so easy!

8-oz. pkg. cream cheese,
  softened
4 c. powdered sugar
1-1/2 t. vanilla extract

12-oz. pkg. white chocolate
  chips
3/4 c. chopped pecans

In a large bowl, beat cream cheese with an electric mixer on low
speed. Gradually add powdered sugar and vanilla; beat until smooth
and set aside. Place chocolate chips in a microwave-safe bowl;
microwave on high for one to two minutes, until melted. Stir chocolate
until smooth; add cream cheese mixture and beat until smooth. Stir in
pecans. Pour into a buttered 8"x8" baking pan. Chill until firm; cut into
squares. Makes about 2 dozen.

Quick Peanut Butter Fudge

Katie Schamle
Hutchinson, KS

No one will know how easy it was to make this awesome treat!

16-oz. can favorite-flavor
  frosting

1 c. creamy or crunchy peanut
  butter

Combine ingredients in a microwave-safe bowl; microwave on high
for 40 seconds. Stir together and pour into a buttered 8"x8" baking
pan. Refrigerate for at least 20 minutes; cut into squares. Makes about
2 dozen pieces.

Black & White Fluff Dessert

Kayla Eubanks
Pensacola, FL

*This oh-so-simple dessert quickly became a favorite of my family &
friends...they ask me to make it often. It just takes a few minutes
and is an easy make-ahead to tuck into the fridge.*

3.4-oz. pkg. instant vanilla
   pudding mix
1 c. buttermilk
8-oz. container frozen whipped
   topping, thawed

1 c. mini marshmallows
20 chocolate sandwich cookies,
   broken

In a bowl, stir together dry pudding mix and buttermilk. Fold in
whipped topping until combined. Stir in marshmallows; carefully fold
in cookies. Chill overnight. Serves 8.

Make up some bite-size ice cream treats just for
the kids...sandwich a scoop of softened ice cream
between vanilla wafers.

Super-Easy Puddin' Cake

Cris Goode
Mooresville, IN

My husband's favorite cake...it's always a hit at get-togethers! The fresh berries make it look special, but it is really simple to make. You can mix & match lots of flavor combinations, like butter pecan cake with butterscotch pudding and topped with pecans, yum! You can even lighten it up a bit with fat-free and sugar-free pudding.

18-1/4 oz. pkg. devil's food
    cake mix
2 3.4-oz. pkgs. instant
    chocolate pudding mix

2 c. raspberries

Prepare cake mix according to package directions. Bake in 2 greased 9" round cake pans; cool. Prepare pudding mixes according to package directions. Place one cake layer on a cake platter; top with half the pudding. Place the other layer on top; cover with remaining pudding. Sprinkle berries on top of cake and serve. Makes 8 servings.

Anchor layer cakes to serving pedestals with a dab of frosting before starting to decorate. The cake will stay in place, making frosting and decorating lots easier!

Secret-Ingredient Turtle Trifle

Brenda Hager
Nancy, KY

*Believe me, your guests will have a hard time guessing that
this quick & delicious dessert started with a frozen pecan pie!*

32-oz. pkg. frozen pecan pie,
   thawed, cut into bite-size
   pieces and divided
8-oz. pkg. cream cheese,
   softened
8-oz. container frozen whipped
   topping, thawed

1 t. vanilla extract
1/3 c. fudge ice cream topping
1/3 c. caramel ice cream topping
1/2 c. chopped pecans

Layer half the pecan pie pieces in a large glass trifle bowl; set aside.
In a bowl, blend cream cheese, whipped topping and vanilla until
smooth. Spoon half of mixture over the pecan pie pieces; repeat
layers. Drizzle with toppings; sprinkle with pecans. Chill before
serving. Makes 15 to 20 servings.

Always serve too much hot fudge sauce on
hot fudge sundaes. It makes people overjoyed
and puts them in your debt.

-Judith Olney

E-Z Chocolate Chip Bars

Jill Gagner
Morris, MN

Made from scratch in just a few minutes! My mom got this recipe from our neighbor when I was growing up. These crunchy bar cookies are always a big hit with my teens and their friends.

1 c. butter, softened
1 c. brown sugar, packed
1 t. vanilla extract

2 c. all-purpose flour
1 to 2 c. semi-sweet chocolate
   chips

Mix butter, brown sugar, vanilla and flour together in a bowl; stir in chocolate chips. Spread into a greased 12"x8" baking pan. Bake at 350 degrees for 20 to 25 minutes, until lightly golden. Cool; cut into squares. Makes one dozen.

Drop off a batch of your favorite cookies to the local firehouse, have the kids deliver them to the teachers' lounge at school or wrap up several and tuck in the mailbox for your letter carrier. What a great way to start the day!

Beckie's Wonder Cookies

Beckie Apple
Grannis, AR

No matter how busy I am, I make time for cooking and baking. These cookies mix up in less than 5 minutes and bake in 8 to 10 minutes... perfect for any busy mom! I named them Wonder Cookies because you'll wonder how they disappeared so fast!

18-1/2 oz. pkg. milk chocolate
   cake mix
1/2 c. butter, melted and slightly
   cooled
1 t. vanilla extract
1 egg, beaten

Optional: 1 c. semi-sweet
chocolate chips, 1/2 c.
chopped nuts, 1/2 c. raisins,
1/2 c. sweetened flaked
coconut

In a large bowl, stir together dry cake mix, butter, vanilla and egg. Fold in optional ingredients, as desired. Form into 2-inch balls and place 2 inches apart on lightly greased baking sheets. Bake at 350 degrees for 8 to 10 minutes, until golden. Makes about 2 dozen.

Crush nuts quickly...place them in a plastic zipping bag
and roll over them with a rolling pin.

Easy-as-Pie Desserts

Simply Peachy Dessert

Libby Case
Shepherdsville, KY

Any time I have church get-togethers, I make this three-ingredient dessert...it's delicious, light and fluffy!

18-1/2 oz. pkg. yellow cake mix   1/2 c. chopped pecans
15-oz. can sliced peaches

Prepare cake mix according to package instructions; set batter aside. Pour peaches and juice into a greased 13"x9" baking pan. Cover peaches with cake batter; sprinkle nuts on top. Bake at 325 degrees for 25 minutes, or until set. Serves 12 to 15.

Cherry Crumb Dessert

Charlotte Smith
Tyrone, PA

Need a quick & easy dessert? Try this...you probably have most of the ingredients in your pantry.

1/2 c. margarine, chilled   1/2 c. chopped walnuts
18-1/2 oz. pkg. yellow cake mix   Garnish: vanilla ice cream
21-oz. can cherry pie filling

In a large bowl, cut margarine into dry cake mix until it resembles coarse crumbs. Reserve one cup of mixture for topping. Pat remaining mixture into the bottom of a greased 13"x9" baking pan and 1/2-inch up the sides to form a crust. Spread pie filling over crust. Combine nuts with remaining crumbs; sprinkle over top. Bake at 350 degrees for 30 to 35 minutes. Serve warm, topped with ice cream. Makes 12 servings.

Caramel Apple Cake

Gloria Robertson
Midland, TX

A scrumptious dessert that feeds a crowd...from only four simple pantry ingredients! Terrific for last-minute potluck invitations.

16-oz. pkg. angel food cake mix   1 t. apple pie spice
21-oz. can apple pie filling   1/2 c. caramel ice cream topping

Mix together dry cake mix, pie filling and spice in a bowl. Pour into a 13"x9" baking pan sprayed with non-stick vegetable spray. Bake at 350 degrees for 30 to 35 minutes. Cool; drizzle with topping. Makes 12 to 15 servings.

Keep a folder for clippings from magazines and newspapers...easy recipes, fun menus and party ideas you'd like to try. Whenever you plan a party, you'll have plenty of great ideas to choose from!

Chocolate Sandwich Cookies

Amanda Porter
North Ogden, UT

These are scrumptious...it's hard to believe they're made from a box of cake mix!

2 18-1/2 oz. pkgs. devil's food
   cake mix
4 eggs, beaten

1-1/2 c. shortening
1 t. vanilla extract

Combine all ingredients in a bowl; mix well. Roll into quarter-size balls and place on greased baking sheets. Bake at 350 degrees for 8 minutes; cool. To assemble cookies into sandwiches, spread Cream Cheese Frosting on the bottom of one cookie; press the bottom of another cookie onto frosting. Refrigerate until ready to serve. Makes about 5 dozen.

Cream Cheese Frosting:

8-oz. pkg. cream cheese,
   softened
1/2 c. margarine

2 c. powdered sugar
1 t. vanilla extract

Blend ingredients well.

Easy-squeezy! Place frosting ingredients in a plastic zipping bag. Squeeze to mix well, then snip off a small corner and squeeze to drizzle over baked goods...just toss away the empty bag!

Candy Shop Pie

Connie Hilty
Pearland, TX

*It's like magic...in just 5 minutes you have a scrumptious dessert
that will really impress everyone!*

1-1/4 c. milk
2 3.4-oz. pkgs. instant vanilla
   pudding mix
8-oz. container frozen whipped
   topping, thawed and divided

4 1-1/2 oz. chocolate candy
   bars, diced and divided
9-inch chocolate cookie crust

In a bowl, combine milk, pudding mixes and half the whipped
topping. Whisk for one minute. Set aside 1/4 cup of candy bar pieces
for garnish. Stir remaining pieces into pudding mixture; spoon into
crust. Spread remaining topping over pie; sprinkle with reserved
candy bar pieces. Serve immediately or refrigerate until ready to serve.
Serves 8.

A quick trick to make chopping candy bars a breeze!
Just wrap them in plastic and freeze for 10 to
15 minutes before chopping.

Easy-as-Pie
Desserts

Frost-Me-Not Cupcakes

Kathy Pounder
El Campo, TX

*My sister-in-law gave me this delicious recipe a long
time ago...such a tasty time-saver!*

4 1-oz. sqs. semi-sweet baking
   chocolate
1 c. butter
1/2 c. chopped pecans

1-3/4 c. sugar
1 c. all-purpose flour
4 eggs, beaten
1 t. vanilla extract

Melt chocolate and butter in a saucepan over medium-low heat. Stir
until smooth; stir in nuts and set aside. In a large bowl, mix together
remaining ingredients by hand; do not beat. Gently fold in chocolate
mixture. Pour into greased or paper-lined mini muffin cups, filling
2/3 full. Bake at 325 degrees for 20 to 25 minutes. Makes 6 dozen.

Toting frosted mini cupcakes to a party or potluck?
Empty egg cartons make clever carriers and
they don't cost you a penny.

201

Sunny Lemon Blossoms

Tina Dillon
Parma, OH

These pop-in-your-mouth treats are addictive!
I only make them when company's coming...so we aren't
tempted to eat them all ourselves!

18-1/2 oz. pkg. yellow cake mix
3.4-oz. pkg. instant lemon
   pudding mix

4 eggs, beaten
3/4 c. oil

Combine all ingredients in a large bowl. Spray mini muffin cups
with non-stick vegetable spray; fill cups 1/2 full with batter. Bake at
350 degrees for 12 minutes. Cool in muffin tin on a wire rack
10 minutes; remove cupcakes from tin and cool completely. Dip each
cupcake into Lemon Glaze to coat; shake off excess. Place on a wire
rack set over a baking sheet; refrigerate until set. Makes 4 dozen.

Lemon Glaze:

4 c. powdered sugar
1/3 c. lemon juice
3 T. lemon zest

3 T. oil
3 T. water

Combine all ingredients; stir until smooth.

Watch for dainty old-fashioned teacups at tag sales.
They're perfect for filling with warm chocolate pudding
or sipping your favorite spiced tea.

Easy-as-Pie Desserts

No-Bake Peanut Butter Bars

*Cheri Maxwell
Gulf Breeze, FL*

*This is a favorite after-school treat at my house. So easy
to make and the kids just love them!*

2 c. margarine, divided
2 c. creamy peanut butter
4-1/2 c. powdered sugar

2 c. graham cracker crumbs
2 c. semi-sweet chocolate chips

Melt 1-1/2 cups margarine and pour into a large bowl. Add peanut
butter, powdered sugar and graham cracker crumbs; blend well.
Spread in a greased 15"x10" jelly-roll pan; set aside. In a saucepan
over low heat, combine remaining margarine and chocolate chips. Stir
occasionally until melted and smooth. Spread over peanut butter layer.
Let cool completely before cutting into bars. Makes 3 dozen.

Host a cookie sampling party! Have each friend
bring a plate of her tastiest cookies, while you provide
the coffee and tea. Such a fun idea for a get-together!

203

Wonderful Wacky Cake

Susan Robinson
Elgin, AZ

When my kids were young, they helped me make this chocolate cake...a delicious homemade dessert in less than an hour.

3 c. all-purpose flour
2 c. sugar
6 T. baking cocoa
2 t. baking soda
1 t. salt

2 c. water
3/4 c. oil
2 t. vanilla extract
2 T. vinegar
Optional: frosting

Sift together flour, sugar, cocoa, baking soda and salt into a large bowl. Add remaining ingredients except frosting; mix until smooth. Pour into a lightly greased 13"x9" baking pan. Bake at 350 degrees for 30 to 35 minutes. Cool; frost if desired. Makes 10 servings.

Creamy Peanut Butter Frosting

Janice Schuler
Alburtis, PA

My mother-in-law used to make this for her son's birthday cakes. She often frosted half the cake with this peanut butter frosting and half with chocolate frosting.

1-1/2 c. powdered sugar
1/2 c. creamy peanut butter
1/4 c. milk

1/2 T. margarine
1/8 t. vanilla extract

Combine all ingredients together in a bowl. Beat until smooth and creamy. Add a little more milk if too thick. Makes enough frosting for a 2-layer cake or one 13"x9" cake.

Easy-as-Pie
Desserts

Pastel Macaroons

Sue Landucci
Endwell, NY

My husband and I found this recipe in a cookbook from the church where we were married nearly forty years ago. My husband is the cookie baker and loves this recipe because it is so easy and tasty. By using different sherbets you can make them any flavors and colors you wish, like raspberry and lime for Christmastime.

2 c. lime sherbet
18-1/2 oz. pkg. white cake mix
1-1/2 T. almond extract

2 7-oz. pkgs. sweetened flaked coconut

Soften sherbet in a large bowl. Add dry cake mix and extract; blend just until well mixed. Stir in coconut. Drop by rounded teaspoonfuls onto greased baking sheets. Bake at 350 degrees for 10 to 13 minutes, until light golden. Makes about 6 dozen.

A melon baller has lots of uses besides making juicy fruit salads. Put it to work forming perfect balls of cookie dough, coring apples and even making pretty little servings of butter for the dinner table. Clever!

Scrumptious Coconut Cake

Melody Taynor
Everett, WA

I just love coconut, but my family refused to eat anything with coconut in it until I found this cake recipe! Now it's everyone's birthday cake and special-occasion cake. The cream of coconut makes it extra-yummy.

18-1/2 oz. pkg. white cake mix
14-oz. can cream of coconut
14-oz. can sweetened
   condensed milk

16-oz. container frozen whipped
   topping, thawed
10-oz. pkg. sweetened flaked
   coconut

Prepare cake mix according to package instructions. Bake in a greased and floured 13"x9" baking pan. When cooled completely, use a wooden skewer to poke holes in the cake. Blend cream of coconut and condensed milk; spoon mixture over cake. Spread topping over cake; sprinkle with coconut. Refrigerate until serving time; keep chilled. Serves 10 to 12.

Make a celebration plate for serving up special treats. Check your local craft store for a clear glass plate and for craft paints designed especially for glass. Along the rim of the plate, add a special message like "Happy Birthday" or "Congratulations." A fun, quick project for all ages.

Easy-as-Pie Desserts

Glorified Grahams

Helen Young
Colorado Springs, CO

A favorite cookie of our three boys and their schoolmates too!
My boys liked to take these cookies to school for classroom
parties...they're easy to carry and yummy to eat.

24 graham cracker squares
1/2 c. butter, melted

1/2 c. brown sugar, packed
1 c. chopped pecans

Arrange graham cracker squares in a single layer on an ungreased
15"x10" jelly-roll pan. Mix together butter and brown sugar in a bowl;
spoon over graham crackers. Sprinkle with nuts. Bake at 350 degrees
for about 12 minutes. Remove to a wire rack. Cool completely; break
into squares. Makes 2 dozen.

For a quick dessert garnish, toast nuts in a small dry skillet.
Cook and stir over low heat for a few minutes, until toasty
and golden. Cool, then place in plastic bags and freeze.
Ready to sprinkle on pies, cakes or ice cream whenever
you want to add a little pizazz!

Cinnamon Buñuelos

Leslie Limon
Jalisco, Mexico

A sweet and easy treat! Buñuelos are a traditional Mexican dessert.
My grandfather prepared them often when I was a child and
now I make them for my own kids.

1 c. sugar	1-1/2 c. oil
1 T. cinnamon	12 flour tortillas

Combine sugar and cinnamon in a bowl; mix well and set aside. In a large skillet, heat oil over high heat. Add tortillas, one at a time, and fry until golden on both sides. Place fried tortillas on a paper towel-lined plate to absorb excess oil. While still warm, dip tortillas in sugar mixture, making sure to coat both sides. Makes one dozen.

Making dessert for a crowd? It's tricky to successfully
double or triple recipe ingredients for cakes, cookies or
candy. Instead, choose a recipe that feeds a bunch,
or prepare several batches of a single recipe until
you have the quantity you need.

Easy-as-Pie Desserts

Mississippi Mud Cake

Suzette Howell
Newcastle, OK

I first tried this fudgy microwave cake back in the early 1980s...it was quick, affordable and the family loved it. I still make it often, just for fun!

1 c. margarine
1/2 c. baking cocoa
4 eggs, beaten
2 c. sugar

1-1/2 c. all-purpose flour
2 t. vanilla extract
2 c. mini marshmallows

Place margarine in a microwave-safe 3-quart casserole dish. Microwave on high until melted, about one minute; cool. Add remaining ingredients except marshmallows; mix well. Microwave on high for 8 minutes, until cake tests done with a toothpick. Sprinkle marshmallows over cake and microwave for one additional minute. Spread Cocoa Icing over warm cake. Makes 12 to 15 servings.

Cocoa Icing:

1/4 c. margarine, melted
2 c. powdered sugar

1/4 c. baking cocoa
1/3 c. milk

In a bowl, blend all ingredients until smooth.

Try this fruit smoothie on a warm day...just substitute milk for water with a favorite frozen fruit juice concentrate. Pour into the blender and blend until frothy. So refreshing!

Hot Fudge Sauce

Jacklyn Akey
Merrill, WI

*Some friends of mine used to serve this luscious Hot Fudge Sauce over
ice cream at all their dinner parties. It was really a hit!*

3 1-oz. sqs. unsweetened
   baking chocolate
5 T. butter

3 c. powdered sugar
1 c. evaporated milk
1 t. vanilla extract

In a saucepan over medium-low heat, melt chocolate and butter.
Remove from heat; stir until smooth. Add powdered sugar alternately
with evaporated milk; blend well after each addition. Return to stove;
bring to a boil over medium heat, stirring constantly. Cook and stir
until sauce becomes thick and creamy, about 8 minutes; stir in
vanilla. Serve warm; refrigerate any leftovers. Makes about 5 cups.

Chocolate Chip Dip

Charlotte Smith
Tyrone, PA

*I make this for all our church socials and ladies' fellowship
meetings...it's always gone, gone, gone!*

8-oz. pkg. cream cheese,
   softened
1/2 c. butter, softened
3/4 c. powdered sugar
2 T. brown sugar, packed

1 t. vanilla extract
1 c. mini semi-sweet chocolate
   chips
graham cracker sticks

In a small bowl, beat cream cheese and butter until light and fluffy.
Add sugars and vanilla; beat until smooth. Stir in chocolate chips.
Serve with graham cracker sticks. Makes 2 cups.

Easy-as-Pie Desserts

German Chocolate Cookies

Jasmine Clifton
Colorado Springs, CO

I created these cookies for my father-in-law, who just loves German chocolate cake. Using cake mix to make cookies gives you big, soft cookies that are so good!

18-1/4 oz. pkg. German
   chocolate cake mix
1/4 c. oil

3 eggs, beaten
14-1/2 oz. can coconut-pecan
   frosting

In a large bowl, combine dry cake mix, oil and eggs. Beat with an electric mixer on medium-high speed until thoroughly blended. Roll into one-inch balls; place one inch apart on baking sheets sprayed with non-stick vegetable spray. Bake at 350 degrees for about 8 minutes, until just starting to set. Immediately remove cookies to a wire rack. Spread with frosting when cool. Store in an airtight container. Makes about 2 dozen.

Yum...bite-size, chocolate-covered bananas! Just slice bananas and dip in melted chocolate. Freeze on a baking sheet, then store in plastic freezer bags, ready to pull out the next time you need a speedy treat.

Chocolatey Chewy Brownies

Jacklyn Akey
Merrill, WI

This recipe reminds me of a family I worked for many years ago.
They're my favorite...the chewiest brownies ever!

1 c. butter, softened
2 c. sugar
4 eggs, beaten
1 c. all-purpose flour

4 1-oz. sqs. unsweetened
   baking chocolate, melted
1 t. vanilla extract
1 c. chopped walnuts

In a bowl, blend together butter and sugar. Add eggs, mixing well. Stir in remaining ingredients. Pour into a greased and floured 13"x9" baking pan. Bake at 350 degrees for 30 minutes. Cool; cut into squares. Makes 1-1/2 to 2 dozen.

Before adding the brownie batter, line your baking pan
with aluminum foil, then grease the foil. Once the
brownies have baked and cooled, they'll lift right out
of the pan, ready to cut in a jiffy.

Easy-as-Pie **Desserts**

Vanilla Layer Cake

Penny Sherman
Cumming, GA

My goodness, is this cake ever easy! I've done a lot of baking in my time, but this is the quickest made-from-scratch cake I've tried. I hope you like it as much as my family and I do!

1-3/4 c. all-purpose flour
2-1/2 t. baking powder
1/2 t. salt
1-1/2 c. whipping cream

1-1/3 c. sugar
2 eggs, beaten
1 t. vanilla extract
Garnish: favorite frosting

In a bowl, mix together flour, baking powder and salt; set aside. In a separate bowl, with an electric mixer on high speed, whip cream with sugar until stiff peaks form. Beat in eggs and vanilla. Fold flour mixture into cream mixture. Pour batter into 2 greased and floured 8" round cake pans. Bake at 375 degrees for 25 minutes, or until a toothpick inserted in center of cake tests clean. Assemble cake with desired frosting. Makes 10 servings.

Mom's Butter Cream Frosting

Hope Davenport
Portland, TX

My mom made this frosting for my birthday cake many times while I was growing up...I still love it! For chocolate frosting, add 1/3 cup baking cocoa along with the powdered sugar.

3-3/4 c. powdered sugar
1/2 c. butter, softened
1 t. vanilla extract

Optional: 1/4 t. almond extract
3 to 4 T. milk

With an electric mixer on medium speed, blend together powdered sugar and butter for about 2 minutes. Add extracts as desired. Stir in milk, one tablespoon at a time; mix until spreading consistency. Makes enough frosting for a 2-layer cake, 2 dozen cupcakes or one 13"x9" sheet cake.

Gooey Butter Cookies

Jill Valentine
Jackson, TN

These cookies are incredible...it's hard to believe they are made from a cake mix! I passed this recipe along to my co-workers. At least once a month someone makes this to share. We can't get enough!

8-oz. pkg. cream cheese,
   softened
1/2 c. butter, softened
1 egg, beaten

1/2 t. vanilla extract
18-1/4 oz. pkg. yellow cake mix
Garnish: powdered sugar

In a bowl, blend together cream cheese and butter; stir in egg and vanilla. Add dry cake mix and blend well; roll into one-inch balls. Roll balls in powdered sugar. Place one inch apart on ungreased baking sheets. Bake at 350 degrees for 10 to 12 minutes or until lightly golden. Remove from baking sheet and cool on a wire rack. Makes 2 dozen.

After a hearty dinner, a simple dessert is perfect. Serve assorted homemade cookies accompanied by scoops of sherbet.

Easy-as-Pie Desserts

Vivian's Mexican Wedding Cake
Jerri Duncan-Shay
Stewartsville, MO

*My mom made this moist cake often for us and we loved it.
When we were first married, my husband ate it often...it was
the only thing I knew how to bake!*

2 c. sugar
2 eggs, beaten
2 c. all-purpose flour
2 t. baking soda

20-oz. can crushed pineapple
1 c. chopped nuts
Optional: cream cheese frosting

Mix together all ingredients except frosting. Pour into a greased 13"x9"
baking pan. Bake at 350 degrees for 30 minutes, until cake tests done.
If desired, frost when cooled. Makes 12 to 15 servings.

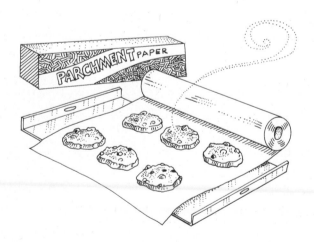

Line baking sheets and pans with parchment paper
cut to fit...cakes and cookies won't stick and
clean-up is oh-so easy.

Best Chocolate No-Bakes

Kimberly Freeman
Springfield, MO

These cookies are my sister's favorite. We don't get to see each other very often, so I always try to have some of these cookies made when I know we'll be getting together.

1/2 c. butter
2 c. sugar
1/2 c. milk
1/4 c. baking cocoa

1/2 c. creamy peanut butter
1 t. vanilla extract
3-1/2 c. long-cooking oats, uncooked

In a saucepan over medium-high heat, combine butter, sugar, milk and cocoa. Bring to a boil; cook for 1-1/2 minutes, stirring frequently. Remove from heat. Stir in peanut butter, vanilla and oats. Drop by teaspoonfuls onto wax paper. Let cool until hardened. Store in an airtight container. Makes 2 dozen.

Dingbats

Louise Andersen
Loves Park, IL

These crunchy, goodie-filled no-bake cookies were a favorite of my sons.

1/2 c. margarine
1 c. sugar
1 c. chopped dates
1 egg, beaten
1 t. vanilla extract

2-1/2 c. crispy rice cereal
2/3 c. chopped nuts
1 to 1-1/2 c. sweetened flaked coconut

In a saucepan over medium-low heat, combine margarine, sugar, dates and egg. Simmer for 5 minutes, stirring constantly. Remove from heat; stir in vanilla. Fold in cereal and nuts. Cool. With buttered hands, form into one-inch balls; roll in coconut. Makes about one dozen.

INDEX

INDEX

INDEX

Snacks & Appetizers

Soups

Find Gooseberry Patch
wherever you are!
www.gooseberrypatch.com

Email

Blog

You Tube

Call us toll-free at 1·800·854·6673

U.S. to Metric Recipe Equivalents

Volume Measurements

1/4 teaspoon	1 mL
1/2 teaspoon	2 mL
1 teaspoon	5 mL
1 tablespoon = 3 teaspoons	15 mL
2 tablespoons = 1 fluid ounce	30 mL
1/4 cup	60 mL
1/3 cup	75 mL
1/2 cup = 4 fluid ounces	125 mL
1 cup = 8 fluid ounces	250 mL
2 cups = 1 pint =16 fluid ounces	500 mL
4 cups = 1 quart	1 L

Weights

1 ounce	30 g
4 ounces	120 g
8 ounces	225 g
16 ounces = 1 pound	450 g

Oven Temperatures

300° F	150° C
325° F	160° C
350° F	180° C
375° F	190° C
400° F	200° C
450° F	230° C

Baking Pan Sizes

Square

8x8x2 inches	2 L = 20x20x5 cm
9x9x2 inches	2.5 L = 23x23x5 cm

Rectangular

13x9x2 inches	3.5 L = 33x23x5 cm

Loaf

9x5x3 inches	2 L = 23x13x7 cm

Round

8x1-1/2 inches	1.2 L = 20x4 cm
9x1-1/2 inches	1.5 L = 23x4 cm